The Mystery of Rommel's Gold

PETER HAINING is a former newspaper reporter, magazine editor and publishing executive who now writes extensively on British history.

He is the author of *The Jail That Went to Sea*, *Where the Eagle Landed* and *The Banzai Hunters* in the *World War II Stories* series, as well as other studies of the Second World War, including the highly praised trilogy, *The Day War Broke Out*, *The Spitfire Summer* and *The Flying Bomb War*. Married with three children and three grandchildren, he lives in Suffolk.

WORLD WAR II STORIES

THE MYSTERY OF ROMMEL'S GOLD
THE SEARCH FOR THE LEGENDARY NAZI TREASURE

PETER HAINING

CONWAY

First published in Great Britain in 2004 by Robson Books, an imprint of Anova Books
Company Ltd.

This paperback edition first published in Great Britain in 2007 by
Conway
an imprint of Anova Books Company Ltd
10 Southcombe Street
London W14 0RA

www.anovabooks.com

British Library Cataloguing in Publication Data
A catalogue record for this title is available from the British Library

ISBN 9781844860531

All the pictures in the plate section are from the author's personal collection, except
p.1 (Anova), p.15 top (Ludovic Maisant/Corbis), p.15 bottom (© Desjobert-Corsica-
Imagebank).

Typeset by FiSH Books, London WC1

Printed by Creative Print & Design, Ebbw Vale, Wales

Cover design by Lee-May Lim

In memory of
Ian Fleming
who introduced me
to the mystery

Contents

Acknowledgements

A great many people have helped me in the writing of this book, a number of whom provided sensitive material and have asked not to be named. Once again I owe thanks to my late friend, Bill Lofts, who devoted several years to looking for clues to the whereabouts of Rommel's gold and collected the photographs used in this book. I am also grateful to Tom Gondris for translations from the German; Pearl Edmunds and Rachel Haining for translating several French texts; and John Kent who provided valuable research from Italy. Bill Wagland was a great help with information about Libya, as was Jonathan Waring about Corsica. The map of Corsica was drawn by Chris Scott, and Nigel Edmunds sketched the elusive *Captain Flint*. Thanks also to Jean-Pierre Joncheray, Robin Leigh, Jean Caubet, Charles Van Deusen, Patricia Lawrence, Brian Willey, Beth Kilmarx, Alfred W McCoy and Al Silverman. My thanks, finally, to Jeremy Robson for commissioning the book and my hard-working editors, Joanne Brooks and Steve Gove, for correcting my mistakes. Any errors of fact are, though, entirely mine.

Author's Note

I should like to make it clear that a few of the names of people mentioned in this book have been changed at their request to preserve their anonymity, or else to protect relatives who are still alive. All of the locations referred to are, however, accurate, as are all the rest of the facts concerning this extraordinary story.

Peter Haining
London, spring 2003

Preface

The Plage de la Marana is a stretch of sandy beach on the east coast of Corsica. It is located a few kilometres to the south of the town of Bastia in the country's Castagniccia region – so named after the chestnut groves that dot the hilly landscape – and has become a favourite water-sports centre in recent years.

Visitors come primarily to sail catamarans or go diving; others come to surf as the area can generate large waves and there are no dangerous rocks in the vicinity. And for those with a taste for history, there is always La Canonica, a twelfth-century Romanesque church on the banks of the River Golo which was built on the site of the ancient city of Mariana, founded in 93 BC.

This bumpy, unexceptional expanse of land belies the history that has been enacted here. Throughout the summer it is baked by the Mediterranean sun that glints off the sea in mazy patterns. Sometimes these rays seem to play tricks, catching the sails of a boat or the bright colours of a catamaran to create little mirages for anyone who is watching.

Several years ago, I holidayed on Corsica with my wife and one of our outings took us to the Plage de la Marana. There we sat one lunchtime having a drink and enjoying plates of the large native oysters, watching the panorama of activities on the sea.

As I looked at one windsurfer, clinging to a huge yellow sail skimming across the water, there was a sudden glint of light just behind the wake of his craft. It looked for all the world like a shaft of gold – the reflection of something just beneath the surface. It was a trick of the light, of course.

Or was it?

I must admit I had a slightly less than altruistic reason for wanting to visit this particular part of Corsica. I had been drawn there because of a story I had heard years before about a hoard of sunken treasure that was supposed to be lying on the seabed just a short distance from the beach. A fortune known as Rommel's Gold.

Of course, it was unlikely that the gold would be visible or that the sun's rays could possibly reflect from it under the sea. But that glint of golden light was surely an omen. At that moment I felt the incentive to try and solve a mystery that had begun during the Second World War, given rise to an enduring legend, and become an all-consuming passion for a diverse yet single-minded group of men and women of various nationalities.

It was to prove a search that would take me from investigating Adolf Hitler's lust for gold, to collecting information about the killing sands of North Africa during one of the crucial campaigns of the war, and a round trip across several of the world's great oceans including the Atlantic, the Mediterranean and the Tyrrhenian Sea – bringing me, ultimately, right back to the same stretch of Corsican coastline.

Preface

The shaft of light from the sea that day – somehow typifying the irresistible allure of gold – gripped my imagination as surely as the thought of Rommel's Gold had gripped all of those whose stories are told in the pages of this book...

1

The Führer's Lust for Gold

The first light of dawn was just breaking over the east coast of Corsica on the morning of 15 September 1943. The sea that lapped on the mile upon mile of sands had been calm during the night and there were no great banks of clouds in the sky to threaten a break in the weather.

Curiously, there was no evidence of activity on the landlocked stretch of water just behind the coast known as the Etang de Biguglia, nor any sign of the fishing boats that would normally be returning to Bastia harbour at this time with their night's catch. Only a solitary boat, a motor launch, was slicing a wake through the dark blue waters as it headed across the last miles of the Tyrrhenian Sea towards the island.

The boat was evidently on a bearing for Cap Sud, situated near the base of Corsica's northernmost promontory that points like an angry, out-thrust finger towards the mainland of Italy. A single figure was evident at the boat's helm, a pair of binoculars clapped to his eyes as he intently studied the approaching coastline.

The navigator had, in fact, just spotted what he believed was the mouth of the River Golo. As he was confirming this fact on a map,

1

an ominous sound broke the early morning silence. The man looked up and a glance was all he needed to confirm his worst fears.

High above, powering in from the south-east, were a group of dark shapes, clear against the brightening sky. At once the navigator shouted to an unseen group in the cabin below and then held his breath as the silhouettes grew ever larger. They were aircraft, obviously: but Luftwaffe or enemy planes?

Even as the thought entered his mind, the man realised it did not matter much either way. Whether friend or foe, they would probably take no chances with a lone boat like his that was flying no flag of nationality and sailing near a front-line island racked by upheaval.

The man swung hard on the wheel of the launch as his three companions spilled into the morning air and gazed up at the sky. As the danger of what they were seeing impacted on their minds, the navigator realised that the sanctuary of the river was the men's only hope of survival if the aircraft attacked.

Barely had the thought crossed his mind when the dark shapes turned into a group of fighter aircraft bearing the white star on a blue background of the US Air Force. They were P-39 Airacobras, one of America's front-line pursuit aircraft which had already built up an awesome reputation in the Mediterranean theatre of war.

The sleek aircraft with its 1,200hp Allison V-1710 engine located behind the cockpit had become a favourite with US pilots and by the time of the attack on Pearl Harbor in December 1941, nearly 600 were in service. Although the P-39's engine was not equipped with a supercharger, it still performed excellently below altitudes of 17,000 feet and was especially good at ground strafing.

Several wings of Airacobras had immediately been assigned to the Northwest African Air Force (NAAF), when it was formed in February 1943 out of a combination of British, Commonwealth and American units, to serve in a joint fighting force under Mediterranean Air Command. The objective of the NAAF was a continuous offensive against the Germans and Italians, accompanied by concerted attacks on enemy airfields so that ground support missions could be carried out free of interference.

The P-39 was especially good at bombing and machine-gun attacks. Capable of speeds up to 376mph and armed with a 37mm cannon that fired through the propeller hub, it also had two 0.5 calibre machine guns and could carry up to 500lb of bombs under its wings. In the hands of a good pilot, it was a truly ferocious fighter.

When the clutch of Airacobras came across the motor launch that September morning they were en route to the port of Bastia, just a few miles further north. This was the boat's destination too.

Ever since the Allies had taken Sicily in July and landed in southern Italy, planes like the P-39 no longer needed to take detours that cut into their range of 650 miles. They could travel on an almost direct flight path from Libya past Sardinia and along the coast of Corsica, where the German–Italian occupation of the island was now rapidly nearing its end.

In fact, both the P-39s and the launch were looking for the same convoy of Axis ships that was in the process of being hastily assembled in Bastia to sail for Italy as soon as possible. To the four men in the boat, this convoy represented the last stage in a cat-and-mouse chase to keep ahead of the advancing Allied forces. For the P-39s, the merchant ships and their escorts amounted to sitting targets.

As the American aircraft passed over the small boat, two of the fighters dropped their speed and peeled away from the group. The remainder headed on up the coast towards their real target.

Instinctively, the man at the helm throttled up every ounce of speed he could conjure from the boat's engine. He knew they had nothing to defend themselves with except a couple of Walther pistols – hopeless against a fighter plane. The only chance was to zigzag as quickly as he could towards the haven of the river estuary.

Behind the boat as it churned the sea feverishly, one of Airacobras levelled off and skimmed in low over the waves, its cannons firing. Spray leapt from the water as the bullets traced an unerring path towards the boat and raked its hull.

Splinters of wood flew, narrowly missing two figures lying prone on the deck. The remaining man had already dived back into the cabin. A flurry of bullets chipped at the bow, while another burst almost tore the navigator from the wheel.

As the first P-39 screamed overhead, it was followed almost immediately by the second, its cannons rattling. Then, as it, too, roared over the boat, a bomb fell from under one wing.

Amazingly, the bomb overshot its target, exploding some yards away but almost submerging the launch with spray. On board, as the vessel rocked from side the side, the four men clung on desperately to the superstructure, praying for their lives.

Whether the pilots of the Airacobras believed they had damaged the boat sufficiently to sink it, or were simply under instructions to continue to their main objective after one foray, both planes immediately began climbing away. Within moments they were heading north in the wake of the rest of the wing.

No one on board the motor launch moved so much as a muscle until they were quite sure the marauders had gone. Nor did they speak a single word to one another until they reached the safety of the banks of the River Golo.

The chipped and scarred woodwork of the boat bore testimony to just how lucky the crew had been to survive. But in their minds they all knew that if the enemy planes were intent on wreaking havoc up the coast where they were also bound, then they had merely survived one narrow escape from death to soon be facing another fate, perhaps even more terrible.

But this was a matter the four men had little time to debate as they contemplated the next stage of their mission – a secret assignment to transport six sealed cases that had begun their journey in North Africa and had already travelled half the length of Italy. They were destined for Germany and, it was believed, ultimately for the Führer himself.

By contrast, it is unlikely that the pilots in the Airacobras even gave a second thought to the boat they had attacked – or could have imagined in their wildest dreams that their unprepossessing target was carrying one of the richest hoards of valuables of the Second World War... the treasure known as Rommel's Gold.

Among the many obsessions nursed by Adolf Hitler during his relentless drive to create a Nazi world order, was a desire to assemble a unique collection of great paintings, objets d'art, jewels, coins and gold. The collection was to be created from the nations conquered by his armies and ultimately assembled in Linz, the industrial town in Austria where he had spent his boyhood. There, the Führermuseum, as it was to be called, would become an immortal monument to his life and achievements. Hitler's dream was to transform his drab home-town into the cultural Mecca of his New Europe, replacing the old one, Vienna, which he despised.

It was during the early years of the twentieth century, while Hitler was living in the Austrian capital struggling to fulfil his ambition to become a great painter, that this ambition was born. His failure to sell his undistinguished watercolours forced him to live in cheap lodgings, begging soup from a nunnery, as his health deteriorated to the point where he became almost consumptive. What Hitler later called 'the most miserable time of my life' only came to an end when the First World War broke out and he was conscripted into the Army.

The poverty and lack of recognition that Hitler suffered in Vienna left him determined to amass the kind of treasures that had made Vienna famous and use these to revenge himself upon the city for failing to recognise his genius. His rapid ascent from rabble-rousing politician to megalomaniac dictator of Germany provided him with the power to achieve this objective. Once he was Führer, his every wish was the command – in most cases the pleasure – of his subordinates.

When Hitler returned in triumph to Linz on 11 March 1938 after ordering his troops into Austria, the ecstatic reception he received from the people who had once been his neighbours made up his mind as to where his Führermuseum should be located. The unremarkable town would be transformed into a modern metropolis with, at its heart a square, colonnaded building greater in size than the Louvre, the National Gallery or New York's Metropolitan Museum. It would house the finest works of art and the richest treasures of Europe – and whatever else of great value the victorious German troops might seize

Hitler instructed one of his favourite architects, Roderick Frick, to draw up plans for the Führermuseum. It was to consist of four buildings, each to house different treasures: one for great works of art, another for arms and armour, a third for rare books and manuscripts and the fourth for rare gold and silver coins, jewellery and objets d'art.

Although the museum was destined never to be completed, the treasure brought to Germany during the war in readiness for filling the massive rooms is believed to have exceeded in value over £1 billion in today's values. As David Roxan and Ken Wanstall have written in their account of this mad dream, *The Jackdaw of Linz* (1964): 'The mass looting of Europe's art treasures by the Nazis was on a scale unprecedented in history – the ancient barbarians preferring to satisfy their lust for destruction rather than acting as common thieves. Looting was carried out with typical German efficiency, planned beforehand and ruthlessly executed.'

To carry out the 'stocking' of the Führermuseum, Hitler ordered the setting up of a special commission, the Sonderauftrag Linz (Linz Special Mission), staffed by trusted officers. The activities of these men were to be classified as secret and all items intended for the museum had to be approved by the Führer himself. Although few references were ever made in public about the mission, Hitler's ambition was known to his senior aides. And those on active service were not slow in realising that to present to the leader special and valuable items seized from battlefield triumphs was a way of ensuring his favour.

Although secrecy surrounded the activities of the Sonderauftrag Linz, documents later captured by the Allies reveal that the group had a number of divisions, all staffed by experts in their respective fields. Hitler chose Munich as the headquarters of the group because the Nazi movement had been born there and it was convenient for the Führer's eyrie at Berchtesgaden. As the collection grew, however, storage space in the city rapidly ran out and new premises were constantly being sought. When the Allied bombing raids began, ever more ingenious hiding places were required, including air-raid shelters, old mine shafts and even deep salt mines.

The man put in charge of assessing the mounds of rare gold and silver coins, jewellery and objets d'art that tumbled into the Mission's offices was Dr Fritz Dworschak. A rather florid-looking man with piercing dark eyes, his job was to sift the bullion, examine and list every item, and then submit these lists – accompanied by photographs – to Hitler for his approval. It was a task that would result in treasure from every corner of the theatre of war appearing for his scrutiny. Few men in history can ever have handled such a fortune as that which passed through his hands in just six years.

Dworschak was himself an Austrian by birth and had studied in Vienna to be an art historian. He had always been fascinated by coins and had obtained the post of Curator of Coins at the Kunsthistorisches Institut. It was following the *Anschluss* (or 'reunification', in Hitler's terms) of his native country that he was recruited for Hitler's special project. If Dworschak knew of his new master's loathing for Vienna – or his intentions to denigrate the great city – he never made mention of the fact.

In fact, Dworschak might well have applauded these emotions because he was already a convert to the Nazi Party and the *Anschluss* brought him rapid promotion. Baldur von Schirach, a high-ranking Nazi administrator, appointed him director of all the collections at the Kunsthistorisches Institut, and he promptly lived up to this seal of approval by sacking anyone who was not pro-Nazi and replacing them with people sympathetic to the cause. When Dworschak was subsequently appointed to the Sonderauftrag Linz his power and influence was extended still further.

It is evident from Dworschak's records that in the early days of his occupation of Austria, Hitler wanted care to be exercised whenever items were being purloined for the Führermuseum. In some instances, it seems, paintings were actually purchased from their owners – though any reluctance was swiftly met with a degree of persuasion – while other items were removed under the pretence they were being 'safeguarded' or 'taken into safe custody'. Only where the owners of collections were Jewish was there no attempt at pretence – the treasures of these unfortunate families were subject to summary *Beschlagnahmt* (confiscation) with no hope of redress or recompense.

According to Roxan and Wanstall this aspect of his job particularly appealed to Dworschak: '[He] took a prominent part in turning the screw with meticulous exactitude, a pastime he readily enjoyed in between his official duties.'

It was not long before the ambitious and hard-working Dworschak was reporting proudly to Hitler that he had seized the immensely valuable coin and medal collections of Leo Furst and Baron Louis von Rothschild, as well as confiscating the collections of no fewer than thirteen religious foundations. A delighted Hitler ordered him to prepare these exceptionally valuable old coins to be housed in a cabinet of their own when the time came.

The immaculate records maintained by Dr Fritz Dworschak reveal that the first officer to curry favour with Hitler with a gift for his museum was the Austrian Gauleiter Buerckel. In December 1939, the unctuous Buerckel dispatched to Berlin a set of medallions depicting the victories of Alexander the Great which he had unceremoniously removed from the mansion of Prince Schwarzenberg in Vienna. A message accompanied the gift: 'I send this gift as a token of my tremendous admiration of, and devotion to, the Führer, whose victories will be even more glorious than Alexander's.'

Buerckel's gift – much appreciated by its vain recipient – puts him first in the line of gift-bearers whose numbers would grow into dozens before the course of the war started to go disastrously wrong and the Führer could no longer be flattered or placated by presents. Hitler's birthday – 20 April – was seized on by a number of other opportunists in the Reich as an excuse to offer him presents, but the ploy was thwarted in many instances by the Führer's right-hand man, Martin Bormann, who had his own agenda for ingratiating himself.

If Hitler had any qualms about the valuables his people were removing from Austria, he had no such reservations when his army overran Czechoslovakia. Army officers and the Waffen SS were given the task of plundering the country's treasure houses and among the items that subsequently found their way back to Munich were the crown jewels of the ancient Czech kings. Large numbers of classic paintings and objets d'art were seized from the homes of prominent Jewish familes, a good many of whom managed to flee the country to avoid their brutal conquerors.

It was the same story in Poland, with vast quantities of art, armour, rare coins, medals, and considerable amounts of the famous Polish silver and gold handiwork being looted from repositories in Warsaw and Cracow. Dworschak notes in his Munich records that 'almost every day wagons are arriving from Poland carrying safeguarded [sic] art objects from public, clerical and private collections.'

The gleam of gold must have been almost blinding and it is no surprise to discover that, such was the volume of items, there were plenty to share out among the other Nazi collectors, notably the Reich Foreign Minister Joachim von Ribbentrop, Propaganda Minister Josef Goebbels and the flamboyant Reich Marshal, Hermann Goering, who secretly nursed an ambition to create his own museum of looted valuables to rival Hitler's on his estate at Karinhall.

When France, too, fell to the German Army, Paris and several other great centres of art were relieved of the choicest items from their collections of paintings, sculpture, tapestries, furniture, enamels, gold and silver – all boxed up and dispatched to Munich for possible inclusion in the Führermuseum. Paris was also home to some of the finest Jewish collections in the world, belonging to the Rothschilds, the Kahns and the Seligmann brothers, as well as the magnificent David-Weill collection of silver and gold, and all became an immediate target of the Nazis.

The consignments of treasure reaching the Sonderauftrag Linz now turned into entire trainloads; historians who have described the marauding Germans at the height of their powers in 1940–41 as 'predatory gangsters terrorising an entire continent as they systematically looted its treasures' are correct in every respect. Indeed, Goering boasted in a letter in November 1940 of the fact that he was not above using the most devious means to boost his coffers: 'I have been able to obtain especially valuable goods from Jewish owners. I obtained them from hiding-places that were very difficult to find. I discovered these by means of bribery and the employment of criminal agents. This activity continues as does the activity of my foreign exchange investigating authorities in scrutinising bank vaults.'

Holland fell to the German Army in May 1940 and similarly suffered the *Beschlagnahmt* and 'safeguarding' of its most precious treasures, although a considerable number of paintings had already been spirited abroad by their owners, alarmed by the stories of what was happening elsewhere. This same summer, of course, Hitler's seemingly unstoppable advance across Europe came to a halt at the English Channel in the face of resolute English defiance and he decided instead to concentrate his forces in Russia.

Evidence suggests that, as in Austria, Hitler would on occasions avoid antagonising the occupied nations and sometimes even paid for items for his collection. Such generosity did not apply to Jewish collections, of course, but certainly there were collectors in Paris and The Hague who made very satisfactory deals with the Führer, albeit that they knew that to refuse the sale was impossible. Occasionally, Hitler was almost generous in the amounts he agreed to pay for classic paintings he especially wanted for the Führermuseum.

However, once the all–conquering Nazi war machine stalled in Russia and then began to fail in North Africa, the Führer's attitude changed completely. There were to be no more deals: he would look to his dutiful officers to provide him with what was needed for the Linz museum – as well as financing the war effort in general – by every means at their disposal.

All this time, Dr Fritz Dworschak had been feverishly busy, examining and submitting descriptions of the golden booty which reached his headquarters. He now had a staff of five coin experts working for him, all sharing his admiration for Hitler and enthused with his determination to make their particular section of the projected museum the best of all.

Dworschak kept a keen eye on the spread of the empire of the Third Reich. His familiarity with numismatic history made him well aware of the locations of the great coin collections and as soon as any of these territories fell into German hands, he was quick to lay claim to their treasure.

Two areas particularly interested him. One was North Africa – home of several rich Jewish dynasties – which was under the control of the Italians, and the other was Italy itself. Mussolini might be the Führer's ally, but the covetous Dr Dworschak suspected that the alliance with the wavering Il Duce might not last. Then, perhaps, some of the ancient civilisation's valuables might be procured to add to the glories already earmarked for Linz?

The possibility of booty from North Africa first impinged on Dworschak's consciousness when Field Marshal Erwin Rommel was assigned to Libya in 1941. The soldier's reputation, forged in the lightning conquest of France, indicated to him that here was a man to whom failure was not an option. As a dedicated Nazi, too, he would surely have no scruples about looting the wealth of those cities and towns he took in the Western Desert.

Dworschak's records indicate that a small battalion of SS officers and men were assigned by von Ribbentrop to work with Rommel and flew to Libya in June 1941. Their brief was to arrange the transport of looted paintings, objets d'art and silver and gold coins back to Germany.

However, instead of this booty being sent to Munich as Dworschak anticipated, it was instead conveyed to von Ribbentrop's headquarters on Hermann Goering Strasse in Berlin. Here it was piled up with vast quantities of valuables that were arriving from Russia – and which eventually spilled out into other places of storage, the whole cache awaiting the attention of the increasingly distracted Führer.

Frustratingly, the records kept by the Waffen SS fall far short of those maintained by Dworschak and his staff and no list has survived to tell us precisely what treasure was looted from North Africa. Nor if there were among these items any that might have been personally selected for Hitler by Rommel himself – that evidence will come from other sources.

In contrast, the story of the Nazis' plundering in Italy after the failure of the Axis alliance has been much better recorded. This began in September 1943 after the Italian resistance to the Allied invasion in the south collapsed, leaving German troops in control of the northern half of the country. Now there was nothing to stop the Nazis taking their pick of the various great collections, especially the magnificent art galleries in Florence.

Accounts of this pillaging of the stricken country's treasures by the retreating German forces have been told in several books, most notably *The Rape of Europa: The Fate of Europe's Treasures in the Third Reich and the Second World War* by Lynn H Nicholas which gives a vivid picture of the complete indifference of

Hitler and his men to the carnage they wreaked on the land of their former ally. The change in the course of the war and the German retreat meant that a considerable amount of this booty fell into Allied hands before it could reach Germany, although a number of other valuable paintings and objets d'art were later to be recovered from their hiding places in German salt mines, at Berchtesgaden and on Reich Marshal Goering's Karinhall estate.

Despite the growing inevitability of defeat, Dr Fritz Dworschak, the dedicated Nazi, stuck to his task of cataloguing the Führer's treasure trove even until just before the Allied forces overran Munich. From the evidence of his record books, one of his final actions was to put together a résumé of the total value of this golden hoard.

By late 1944, the majority of these items unlikely now ever to be displayed in the fanciful Führermuseum, were being stored in a salt mine at Alt Aussee. The largest area was occupied by almost 10,000 paintings, of which over half were old masters. There were also 128 items of armour, over 120 crates filled with objets d'art, and 32 cases of gold and silver coins. To the group of American soldiers who first entered the mine, it must have seemed as if they had stumbled upon Aladdin's fabled cave.

Thereafter followed years of painstaking work by the Allies – the Americans in particular – among this treasure in order to return the looted artefacts to their rightful owners. Even when this daunting task was eventually brought to a close some six years later, there were still many items that remained unidentified.

The ownership of coins, in particular, was especially hard to determine as they were of such varied countries of origin and dates. However, one small bag caught the eye of Captain Robert Possey, a member of a group of servicemen-detectives known as the Art Looting Investigation Unit of the US Office of Strategic Services. It was initialled 'E.R.' and contained a curious mixture of Arab and Jewish coins.

Although these coins – and all the others in the 32 cases – were soon removed from the dank vault in Alt Aussee, the US captain could not get the little bag out of his mind. Why should the currency of two such implacable enemies be found together? Where had they come from? And, most important of all, what or who did the initials 'E.R.' stand for?

Possey and his colleagues in the Art Looting Investigation Unit later produced a series of reports on their work. These documents were circulated to a select group of military and civil bodies, with copies of each being deposited in the National Archives of the State Department in Washington. The reports leave almost as many questions unresolved about the Nazi gold hunt as they answer.

This has not, though, stopped speculation about the whereabouts of some of the treasure trove that is still missing in Germany and elsewhere – or the origin of mysterious little caches like that inscribed 'E.R'. Indeed, after some years of deliberation, 'Detective' Possey thought he might have the solution. Could the initials stand for Erwin Rommel, and might the mixture of coins have been part of the loot seized by the Field Marshal's men during their triumphant passage acros North Africa?

Good detective as he undoubtedly was, Robert Possey was mistaken in trying to make a connection with Rommel; the initials were in all probability a designation given by Dr Fritz

Dworschak. In truth, the American could have no idea how much more complex was the story of Rommel and the treasure bearing his name...

There are many variations of the legend of Rommel's Gold. In the half century since the story first emerged about a vast wartime fortune in valuables lying somewhere in the Mediterranean awaiting discovery, it has become the source of a great deal of speculation and rumour. There is rather more ✗ fantasy than fact attached to the legend, and it is my intention in this book to try and examine them both and establish once and for all the location of the lost hoard.

It is interesting first, though, to consider the most popular accounts of the treasure and its association with the German Field Marshal Erwin Rommel, 'The Desert Fox'. The hoard is variously said to consist of four or six carefully sealed cases. They weigh anything up to two and a half tons and contain gold ingots, gold and silver coins, diamonds, jewellery, precious stones and objets d'art. The value of the cache has variously been estimated at anything between £6 million and £60 million.

According to one of the most frequently repeated stories, Rommel collected a great treasure in gold, silver and precious artefacts during his initially very successful campaign in North Africa. As a devoted admirer of Hitler – who, it was said, had taken a personal interest in his career – Rommel decided to send this hoard to Germany as a gift for the Führer. But the vessel carrying the gold never reached its destination.

A variation of this account claims that Rommel had no such altruistic motives and actually believed that Hitler would ultimately lose the war. It was while he was retreating from the

Allied troops across Libya that he decided to send the booty by U-boat to Corsica. The submarine reached the island, the valuables were unloaded and then carefully hidden. But, so the story goes, as the submarine left the island it was seen by an American bomber, a B-17 Flying Fortress, which attacked and sank the vessel. With the loss of the U-boat went all knowledge of the whereabouts of the Field Marshal's treasure.

A third account adds confusion to the route of the treasure. It suggests that far from being a gift destined *for* Hitler, the gold was actually on its way *from* Germany to Rommel to be used as funds to pay his men and advance his campaign in North Africa.

A fourth story maintains that Rommel's hoard was seized by a group of renegade Afrika Korps soldiers led by an officer known only as Schmidt who hid it in the Libyan desert. The men apparently planned to return to the area after the war and reclaim the fortune. Although attempts have subsequently been made to find it, no trace has come to light.

The rumour mill has also claimed that the treasure was deliberately sunk by a German vessel in 30 fathoms of water in the bay of Bastia; or, alternately, that the gold was quietly being shipped back to Germany in a merchant ship via neutral Spanish ports when it went missing somewhere along the way.

Not surprisingly, the legend of Rommel's Gold has attracted the interest and energies of a very varied group of people, many of whom feature in the pages of this book. Some have simply researched the story, others have actually gone in search of the hoard: a few have paid for the experience with their lives.

There have been famous personalities involved in the story. People like Ian Fleming, the creator of James Bond, and Edwin Link, inventor of the Link trainer and a pioneer of underwater exploration. Not forgetting more notorious characters including the Scottish safe-cracker, Johnny Ramensky, and the elusive German fortune hunter, Peter Fleig. All of them united by a fascination with gold – and the story of the Field Marshal's missing treasure in particular.

The mystery of Rommel's Gold is as full of twists and turns as any classic thriller story. It is a tale of obsession, violence, criminal activities and the murder of some of those who may have come too close to the truth of its whereabouts. The difference is that this story is true.

2

The Spymaster in Mitre Court

The first time I heard about the legend of Rommel's Gold was forty years ago in an unobtrusive little office just off Fleet Street, then the heart of London's newspaper industry. The man who told me about the mysterious hoard was Ian Fleming, journalist, bon viveur and creator of the most famous spy in literature, James Bond, Agent 007.

Fleming, himself a former intelligence officer, was by the winter of 1963 a best-selling author on both sides of the Atlantic, his creation James Bond well on his way to becoming one of the icons of the twentieth century. However, a little-known fact about Ian Fleming then – and probably still among the least appreciated elements of his fame today – was that he had a lifelong passion for treasure hunting.

As a child, Fleming loved going in search of lost hoards of valuables like those described in his favourite novels by Robert Louis Stevenson and Rider Haggard – and as an adult working on the *Sunday Times*, he co-ordinated several hunts for famous caches of gold which had been suggested as possible targets by the newspaper's readers. These explorations provided both a circulation boost to the *Sunday*

Times and a breath of excitement for the desk-bound Ian Fleming.

Among the lost treasures suggested to the paper was the missing fortune known as Rommel's Gold. It might still lie hidden in North Africa or else on the bottom of the Mediterranean Ocean, according to one reader whose letter reached Fleming's desk. Although the evidence offered for the location of the treasure was singularly vague – and any idea of organising a search for it clearly beyond the time and resources available to the *Sunday Times* – the bare facts of the fabulous hoard grabbed Fleming's interest; all the more so because during his work as an intelligence officer, North Africa had been for a time one of the main focal points of his information gathering.

Fleming, I was to learn, was a man who made good use of every scrap of information that came his way during the war years and later as a journalist – especially when it came to providing the adventures of James Bond with their remarkable sense of authenticity. Indeed, there is no reason to doubt the statement of John Pearson, author of the biography *The Life of Ian Fleming*, that the novels are 'the undercover autobiographies of Ian Fleming' – or to be surprised that he referred to Rommel's Gold in one of the best of the series, *On Her Majesty's Secret Service*, published in April 1963.

Certainly, the mystery was still on the author's mind when we met some eight months later. Our conversation that December was to provide material for an article I was preparing about him and the James Bond phenomenon – and, in the fullness of time, to inspire the writing of this book.

The search for the origins of Ian Fleming's fascination with the legend took me via the Fleming family home, his secret intelligence work at the Admiralty in London, and his period as a globe-trotting journalist and best-selling author. Most crucial of all, was the meeting in that little office in Mitre Court.

Ian Lancaster Fleming was born on 28 May 1908, the second of four sons of Major Valentine Fleming, Conservative MP for South Oxfordshire, and his wife, Evelyn, considered by many people of the time as one of the most beautiful women of her generation. Major Fleming won a DSO while serving in the First World War, but was killed in action in May 1917, leaving his wife and children to grow up in the shadow of a dead hero. A copy of the generous tribute to Major Fleming written by Winston Churchill for *The Times* a few days after his father's death hung on the wall of Ian Fleming's home throughout his life.

Despite this tragedy, the Fleming children still had a very influential grandfather to emulate: a Scottish millionaire who had created his own private bank, Robert Fleming & Company in the City of London, and used his wealth to erect a huge mansion, Joyce Grove, at Nettlebed near Henley-on-Thames. It was in this opulent house that young Ian Fleming grew to appreciate the value of money and in the sprawling, tree-lined grounds that he first played the 'games of initiative' that characterised much of his later life.

There is evidence that the boy's passion for treasure hunting began as early as the age of nine. According to John Pearson, while on holiday with his mother and brothers at St Ives in Cornwall, Fleming went searching for amethyst crystals and deep in one cave found a lump of greyish-yellow paste which he decided was a piece of ambergris.

'It was as big as a child's football and I knew it was ambergris from one of the adventure books I had been reading,' he was to write later. 'Now I would be rich and I would be able to live on Cadbury's milk chocolate and I would not have to go back to my private school or indeed do any more work at all.'

As Fleming carried his 'prize' back to the hotel where the family were staying, something strange began to happen. When he at last found his mother and proudly offered her the dripping lump, he was greeted with a shocked look and a demand for an explanation as to what it was.

'It's ambergris,' Ian said, wiping sticky hands on his jumper. 'Do you know, it's worth a thousand pounds an ounce and there must be two pounds of it!'

A member of the hotel staff, standing quietly behind Mrs Fleming and wrinkling his nose, shattered the boy's dream of wealth: 'I am afraid it is rancid butter, Madam, probably from the New Zealand supply ship that was torpedoed off the coast a few months ago!'

The humiliating experience did not, however, cure Ian Fleming of his obsession with treasure hunting.

After a period of private schooling at Durnford in Dorset, Fleming was sent to Eton where he excelled at athletics rather than academic subjects. Instead of going to university, the restless young man opted for the Royal Military College at Sandhurst. Here he soon grew tired of the routine and endless drill of army life and was sent by his mother to a private college in Kitzbühel to improve his developing facility for languages, German in particular. It was intended that Fleming should sit the entrance examination for a place in the Foreign Office, but the indications are that the darkly handsome young man devoted more time to writing poetry and short stories as well as improving his facility at seduction.

In 1929, Fleming spent a year in Munich as a less than dedicated student at the university. Curiously, although this city was then the headquarters of the burgeoning Nazi party and a certain rabble-rouser named Adolf Hitler, the young Britisher seemed unaware of either and certainly did not mention the turmoil in Germany in any of his letters home. Nor, for that matter, did he mention any of the girls he charmed into his bed.

That same year, in late July, he joined his mother and three brothers for their annual holiday, this year to Corsica. The party travelled by ship from Nice to Bastia and Ian Fleming fell in love with the place at once. He took to swimming five or six times a day in the sea, becoming ever more fascinated by the marine life and the many unusual formations on the sandy bottom of the bay. He could have had no idea that this very spot would soon feature in the most extraordinary of treasure hunts.

Perhaps unsurprisingly, because of his indolence in Kitzbühel and Munich, Fleming failed to gain a position in the Foreign Office and in 1931 was forced to look for another occupation. He had, of course, already done a little writing and so, aided by his mother's contacts in the right circles, applied for a job in the London office of Reuters news agency.

Much to his delight, Fleming was offered a job in the newsroom. He took with great energy and enthusiasm to his duties of working on the reports that came in from all corners of the world and in later years was to acknowledge his debt to the agency for helping to shape his writing style and his ability to gather facts.

In March 1933, Fleming was sent by Reuters to their Moscow bureau and there at first hand saw the elements of Russian life that would directly inspire the Bond novels. A colleague from that time, Geoffrey Bocca, recalled in 1964 in an interview with the *Sunday Times*: 'Ian may have been young and a bit green, but already one could see the older, ever-curious Fleming peeping out. Many correspondents hated Moscow, but he loved it and quickly added Russian to his fluent German and French. He was also fascinated by the Russian secret police who were everywhere.'

That spring he came face to face with some of these sinister figures when he covered the trial of six British engineers working in Russia for the Metropolitan-Vickers Company. They were charged with plotting against the Soviet state by sabotaging machinery and installations at power stations and factories and bribing Russians for secret information. In a word, spying.

Reporting the trial introduced Fleming to the world of OGPU, the Russian secret police, and their use of violence and torture to extract confessions. The disclosures made a deep impression on him – as well as convincing him that the whole trial was a sham. The reports he filed to London were models of concise information and in them can be seen developing the style so well executed in the 007 novels – not to mention the origins of the brutal worlds of SMERSH, SPECTRE and their brainwashed employees.

Ian Fleming was, then, seemingly on the verge of a glittering career at Reuters – with the prospect of a plum job as the company's Far East correspondent based in Shanghai – when he suddenly opted for the more golden opportunity, financially speaking, of a job in merchant banking. He had never forgotten the opulence of his grandfather's lifestyle and when he was offered the chance of a position in the merchant banking firm of Cull & Co. in Bishopsgate – the influence of the family name no doubt playing some part in this offer – he quit Reuters with the minimum of fuss or explanation.

It soon became apparent, however, that Ian Fleming had not inherited his grandfather's ability to earn a fortune. His stated intention of 'making a great deal of money and living on my own terms in considerable comfort' did not match his performance as a stockbroker – even when he joined a larger firm, Rowe & Pitman, a year later – and by 1939, with the clouds of war gathering on the horizon, he was still as far away from achieving his ambition as when he had begun.

However, the outbreak of the Second World War was unexpectedly to provide the opportunity for yet another career change. A change that would once again stimulate his passion for treasure hunting and ultimately lead to the pot of gold embodied in a secret agent named James Bond.

Room 39 in the West Block of the Admiralty building on Whitehall was to be where Ian Fleming spent much of his time during the war years. This old-fashioned, high-ceilinged, ground-floor room with its views across Horse Guards Parade was the nerve centre of the Naval Intelligence Division under the command of Rear Admiral John Henry Godfrey.

How Fleming found himself in these surroundings was largely due to some work he had carried out earlier for the British Secret Intelligence Service. It was an aspect of his life that remained clothed in secrecy until the release a few years ago of classified wartime information restricted by the Official Secrets Act.

Fleming had, as we know, tried unsuccessfully to join the Foreign Office in 1931. He had, however, apparently come to the attention of the men in Whitehall two years later through his reporting of the trial of the Metropolitan-Vickers engineers. On his return from Russia, he was approached by Foreign Office officials and in a series of interviews provided his impressions of the country, in particular the secret police.

In 1939, Fleming was asked to return to Moscow once again: ostensibly as a special correspondent for *The Times* covering the British Trade Mission to Russia, but in reality under orders from the Foreign Office's Military Intelligence, Section 6 (MI6) to assess the Soviet Union's security precautions and military strength. The indications are that he returned with invaluable data about the protection of the Kremlin and the attitude of the Russian leadership towards what was already being regarded as an inevitable war with Germany.

Not long after this, Fleming found himself an object of attention from the famous 'old boy' network in London when he was 'invited by someone who knew someone' – in fact a brother of one of the partners in Rowe & Pitman – to lunch with Rear Admiral Godfrey. The donnish former captain of HMS *Repulse* was on the lookout for intelligent, talented young men from a diversity of occupations to work in Section 17 of the Naval Intelligence Division, to which he had just been appointed. If, as expected, war broke out, Rear Admiral Godfrey and his team would be responsible for collecting and sifting every scrap of information about the enemy's plans that might affect the British Navy.

There is no doubt that the decisive and far-sighted Rear Admiral and the young stockbroker cum journalist cum part-time spy took an immediate liking to one another. On 26 July, Ian Fleming was appointed Lieutenant (Special Branch) in the

Royal Naval Volunteer Reserve and took up the position of personal assistant to the Director of Naval Intelligence. Just how highly the boss of the NID came to rate his PA may be judged from this comment made years later: 'He [Fleming] had a remarkable power of assimilating the details of any organisation and I arranged for him to be shown everything. Within a month he had a better all-round picture of Naval Intelligence and its place in the Admiralty than most of the people who had been there for years.'

Once Britain was at war, Fleming took to his new duties like a duck to water – clearly a man who had found a job to which he was ideally suited. To his natural charm and imaginative thinking he had added an air of confidence and authority (if not wealth) from his years in the City. In company with Godfrey's twenty men and women in the cramped conditions of Room 39, he got on with the business of deciphering seized documents and maps, cracking codes, monitoring German radio broadcasts, pinpointing the position of enemy vessels via aerial reconnaissance, interrogating spies and communicating with agents who had infiltrated Occupied Europe.

Fleming's role made him privy to all the top secret information that came Rear Admiral Godfrey's way and he frequently liaised with other departments about matters of propaganda, subversive activities (suggesting, on one occasion, the printing of forged German banknotes 'to attack Nazi currency and enrage the Germans') and even political warfare. He also acted as the conduit of information to MI6, the Special Operations Executive (SOE) and the US Navy Intelligence Bureau in Washington. On other occasions he carried out a variety of unofficial and unorthodox tasks as part of the licence to act on his own initiative that Godfrey had granted him.

In a word, Fleming became a fixer par excellence of people and activities, rapidly earning promotion to Lieutenant Commander and then full Commander. He also continued to mix with the rich and powerful of London and assiduously devoted himself to picking up any gossip or inside information that might be of use. Some of the naval officers in the Admiralty, observing the civilian PA's ascendancy, seemingly grew jealous and nicknamed him 'The Chocolate Sailor'.

There was nothing soft-centred about Ian Fleming, however, and in 1940, after becoming increasingly concerned about German activities in the Mediterranean, he put forward a plan of action to prevent Spain from allowing the Germans to install radar equipment and infra-red cameras in the Straits of Gibraltar. He believed that this could seriously jeopardise the Navy's Mediterranean strategy and proposed a joint operation with the SOE. The plan was to immobilise Spain's ports and give other assistance in case the Germans attacked neutral Spain and ultimately Gibraltar.

Although nothing came of this proposal – filed as 'Operation Golden Eye' – Fleming never forgot the code name and later adapted it for the holiday home he built in Jamaica. Despite the pressures of his job, the allure of gold still haunted Fleming's thoughts.

His interest in buried treasure surfaced again during the terrible months of the Battle of the Atlantic when Britain depended on supplies of arms, munitions and food from America for her survival. He knew that there were a number of sunken ships around the British Isles – and because of the record number of German strikes, wondered whether the enemy might have installed listening devices in some of these wrecks to transmit the engine noise of passing Allied shipping to their U-boats.

The evidence suggests that the Admiralty took the idea seriously enough to order a detailed search of the wrecks known to be lying along the Kent coast. Nothing was found – but no one could argue that Fleming's idea was totally improbable.

Another idea which no one – except the Germans – was supposed to take seriously also emanated from Fleming's fascination with accounts of treasure hunting. During some expeditions in the past, he had read, a number of fortune hunters had resorted to an ancient superstition that claimed the location of a lost cache could be found by swinging a pendulum over a map.

According to historian Leonard Thomason, German Naval Intelligence picked up on this idea and actually employed several astrologers to see whether it was possible to use the concept to locate the routes of Allied shipping for their U-boats to attack. He told John Pearson:

> Fleming used occult contacts outside the NID to plant this fake information on the German Navy. The enemy were led to believe the NID were also employing pendulum predictors at the Admiralty to scan charts and find the position of U-boats. At that time Britain's increased success in sinking U-boats with more effectively set depth-charges caused the Germans to believe Fleming's fabrication. With the bait taken, the German Naval Command persisted in their attempt to discover the pendulum method through application and extensive research experiments.

It might be concluded from this that Ian Fleming's childhood passion for hidden gold had achieved an unlikely victory!

In mid-June 1940, just before the fall of Paris, Fleming was briefly freed from the confines of the Admiralty for a dash across the Channel to retrieve a large quantity of secret papers that had been left behind in the British Embassy in Bordeaux. Not only was he successful, but he also arranged the evacuation on a neutral ship of a number of wealthy British expatriates along with King Zog of Albania, who was fleeing the continent with his family and the country's famous crown jewels.

The following February, Fleming was given leave from the Admiralty once again and dispatched to North Africa on a secret mission. His destination was Tangier and to ensure his safety he was issued with a special courier's passport, a commando fighting knife and a fountain pen complete with cyanide cartridge.

Tangier was then one of the major centres used by MI6 to spread false information to the German and Italian Intelligence groups through the use of double agents. Fleming's brief was to check on Naval Intelligence throughout North Africa. He found the atmosphere in the neutral city rife with rumours about what was going on in the neighbouring occupied countries of Tunisia and Libya.

As Fleming made his way around the hotels and restaurants meeting one contact after another, word reached him that a new German general was expected to arrive in Libya any day to take command of the combined German and Italian military forces.

He did not need the expertise of the men back in Room 39 to tell him that the man was Field Marshal Erwin Rommel, fresh from his triumph in France. Fleming sensed at once that the man would prove a tenacious foe – but never suspected that he would later hear the German's name in connection with a vast hoard of treasure.

Fleming made the most of this brief escape from office duties to see the city and have some fun. He spent one particular night on the town with a young British attaché, Henry Greenleaves, during which they got uproariously drunk, broke into the local bullring, and drew a 20-foot-wide 'V' sign in the sand. The incident caused a minor diplomatic row – and for one of the few occasions during his time as PA to Admiral Godfrey, Fleming returned home to London to receive a sharp reprimand from his superior.

That same year Fleming visited America to liaise with the US Navy Intelligence Department. On this trip he met the Canadian-born businessman turned spymaster, Sir William Stephenson, known by the code name 'Intrepid'. Stephenson had been busy building up the British Intelligence network throughout North and South America and Fleming was instantly impressed by the man's patriotism and single-minded dedication to his task – and the fact that he served the largest dry Martinis in America.

During his time with Stephenson, Fleming was taken to the millionaire's isolated farm on the shore of Lake Ontario where his agents were being trained in the arts of subversion and sabotage. Fleming took the opportunity to learn about unarmed combat, safe-blowing, survival techniques and the planting of explosives. His ability as a swimmer enabled him to do well at an exercise which required him to swim undetected underwater and attach a limpet mine to the hull of a derelict tanker moored on the lake.

Throughout the summer of 1942, the team in Room 39 were kept busy with the plans for the invasion of North Africa by Anglo-American forces. The tactics of Field Marshal Rommel and his Panzer troops had proved hugely successful and it was now imperative for the Allies to prevent him entering Egypt and taking the vital Suez Canal.

Fleming played an important organisational role behind the invasion, setting up and training a small unit of 'Intelligence Commandos' whose mission was to go in with the troops and then scavenge for all the enemy information they could find. Referred to as Number 30 Assault Unit (30AU) they were intensively trained in the same tough style devised by Sir William Stephenson in Canada. Fleming came to refer to this group with a proprietorial air as his 'Red Indians'.

When 30AU landed on the coast of North Africa at Sidi Ferruch to the west of Algiers on 8 November 1942, they had been well provided with detailed maps and reconnaissance photographs. Not being part of the main assault force, however, they had to improvise their own transport, but struck pay dirt when they found the villa on the outskirts of the city that the Italians had been using as their naval headquarters.

The half dozen men fell eagerly upon the files and code books that the surprised Italians had not had time to burn. By the following day a mass of information – including the battle orders of the German and Italian fleets and the enemies' current ciphers – was on its way by top priority via Gibraltar to Room 39 in the Admiralty.

From the code books, technical files and fighting procedures that arrived in Whitehall, Godfrey's team were able to provide invaluable information for the British and American forces as they scoured the Mediterranean for enemy ships and fought their way along the hostile coast of North Africa. Among other crucial pieces of information discovered by 30AU were the Germans' latest designs for minefields and defences that made the later Allied invasion of Sicily a less hazardous operation.

In the wake of the advance of the Anglo-American forces as they moved eastwards to meet up with the Eighth Army under the command of Lieutenant-General Bernard Montgomery in April 1943, Fleming set up an Intelligence network to collect every scrap of information it could from captured German troops and liberated civilians. The titbits of rumour and gossip that were picked up from these sources told the NID a lot about the behaviour and morale of the German and Italian soldiers as Rommel's great triumph at Tobruk turned into a humiliating retreat from the borders of Egypt all the way back to Tunisia.

Stories also reached Fleming's ears about looting by German soldiers in the cities they had captured. In the main they concentrated on food, ammunition and weaponry. Although this in itself was no surprise – conquering armies have always allowed themselves the spoils of victory – the wealth of North Africa was known to subsist primarily in precious metals, coins, jewellery and objets d'art and a file was opened in Room 39 to list any caches that might come to Allied attention. If, however, Rear Admiral Godfrey's team heard anything of the stories of Rommel's Gold at this time, there is no mention of it among the papers in the file.

Commander Ian Fleming was to make one more valuable haul of material before the war came to an end. John Pearson has written: 'As the invading armies stormed their way into Germany both the Americans and the British were trying to snatch whatever secrets they could from the ruins of the Third Reich. The treasure hunters had reached the treasure, but everything depended on knowing where to look and what to look for; and Fleming's Black List of wanted enemy equipment became the catalogue for 30AU's final shopping list.'

The very last of these 'shopping trips' occurred just before the German surrender on 7 May 1945, when rumours reached the NID that plans were being made by Hitler loyalists to destroy a huge amount of secret material stored at Tambach Castle in Bavaria. Fleming with three of his 'Red Indians' raced off to the location.

At the site, the party found three men busy piling case after case of documents into a giant pile in the dried-out bed of a lake. They were clearly intent on setting fire to the papers that Fleming discovered were the complete German Naval Archives dating back to 1870. The stacks of material, weighing several tons, proved so bulky that he had to charter a fishing ship to take them from Hamburg back to London for examination. Commander Fleming was, for once, not sorry that the onerous task of cataloguing and filing this immense amount of material did not fall to his responsibility.

There is probably some truth in the story that after his release from the Royal Navy in November 1945, Ian Fleming continued for a time to be involved with the world of Intelligence gathering. He certainly met with Sir William Stephenson on several occasions and may well have discussed the idea of a career in either MI5 or MI6.

Equally, it is known that he became friendly with Allen Dulles, the Director of the CIA, who was always looking for men with practical experience like Fleming for his network of 'spooks' – all the more so when the Cold War with Russia became more hostile. Rear Admiral Godfrey also created a club of ex-Intelligence officers who could be re-employed in the event of trouble with Russia and his former second-in-command was certainly among their number.

Whatever the extent of his involvement in espionage, Fleming was lured back into journalism by Lord Kemsley who offered him the job of organising a foreign news service for his chain of national and provincial newspapers, in particular the *Sunday Times*. Fleming's quick wit, intelligence, nose for a story and wide circle of society friends, plus all the contacts he had made during the war years, enabled him to fill the post with admirable skill. The 'Fleming Network' was one that became widely admired – and envied – by his colleagues at Kemsley Newspapers.

According to another of Fleming's biographers, Andrew Lycett, Ian was still so full of the romantic image of Tangier as 'a centre of espionage and skulduggery' that he dreamed up a plan for purchasing the small *Tangier Gazette* and turning it into an English-language newspaper serving the Mediterranean. He even gained the backing of Lord Kemsley, but sadly the project came to nothing.

A singularly generous clause in Ian Fleming's contract with Kemsley enabled him to take two months leave every year to go to his holiday home, Goldeneye, at Oracabessa on the north coast of Jamaica. Here he spent his time writing and snorkelling among the reefs in the bay in front of his property. Though Fleming never expected to find anything more exotic than the occasional glittering piece of rock or coral, dreams of treasure hunting were never far away as he swam leisurely through the crystal-clear waters that had once been the haunt of pirates and buccaneers.

In 1952, after years of hedonistic bachelorhood, Fleming finally married Ann Rothermere, the former wife of another London newspaper proprietor. The event was to prove a cathartic moment in his life as his long-time friend and *Sunday Times* colleague, Godfrey Smith, recalled in a *Sunday Times* column in 1974: 'It was to get used to the shock of marriage that Ian went to Goldeneye and wrote his first thriller, *Casino Royale*, in just seven weeks, pounding his old-fashioned typewriter for three hours each morning between his swim and his siesta. I know he disclaimed any similarities between himself and 007, but there were plenty. Both were naval officers, both were *aficionados* of food, drink, cars and women; and both knew the seamier side of the world's great cities.'

Biographer Andrew Lycett is also very pertinent on this moment in his subject's life: 'James Bond was the man of action he would like to have been, if his nature had not been more passive, reflective and chameleon-like. More prosaically, Bond gave at least fictional form to Ian's frustrated urge to have been out in the field during the war, a full-time secret agent, rather than a competent officer sitting, office-politicking and dreaming, in room 39 of the Admiralty.'

By the time I met Ian Fleming in December 1963, his total of ten James Bond novels had sold in excess of 20 million copies and the first two movies, *Dr No* and *From Russia With Love*, had been filmed with Sean Connery. Each book took him between two and three months to write and they appeared, regular as clockwork, each Easter. The success of the novels had enabled him to give up his job at Kemsley in 1960 – although he continued to contribute to the *Sunday Times* until his death – and to set up his own little office as the hub of Bond Enterprises – or Glidrose Productions, to give the limited company into which his earnings poured its correct name.

The premises were located at the top of Fleet Street in Mitre Court, a quiet and sedate haven mostly occupied by legal firms. From the courtyard, a short stairway led up to a pair of rooms, one occupied by Fleming and the other by his efficient and formidable secretary, Beryl Griffie-Williams, who had previously worked for two other authors, Rebecca West and Nancy Spain.

Fleming's room, I remember, was elegant with green, Regency-striped wallpaper and a single, small-paned window. In the middle was positioned a solid antique desk with a green leather top behind which he sat smoking one of his endless Morland's Special cigarettes in an ebonite Dunhill holder. The one incongruous item on the desk was a quill pen acquired during his days in Room 39 that now took pride of place beside an ashtray.

On the walls hung pictures of several half-naked girls – the artwork for the dust jackets of the American editions of the Bond books. Similarly eye-catching was a glass-fronted oak bookcase in which I was surprised to see a number of paperback copies of the hardboiled novels of Raymond Chandler and Mickey Spillane as well as three books by Jacques Cousteau, the famous French underwater explorer, dealing with his deep-sea diving exploits. It was not until we had talked for a while that I came to appreciate the significance of the Cousteau titles.

The author was dressed, as he invariably was, in a dark blue suit with a polka-dot bow tie. His hair was still dark and wavy, though greying around the ears, and his slightly hooded, pale blue eyes had a habit of smiling sardonically whenever he was amused by something. Although only 55, his fleshy face bore all the evidence of hard-won experience and I could sense what his friends meant when they said the Bond books were drawn from his own life and full of characters 'dredged up from his past'.

Our conversation was, initially, about his life and the creation of James Bond which he discussed with the practised ease of someone who has told the same story to interviewers many times before. It was only when we got on to his home in Jamaica – to which he would shortly be going – that he became more animated. It was clearly the place where he was happiest and where he did his best writing. It was also, he said, where he could indulge his passion for underwater swimming and exploration.

I told him I had been intrigued to see the Jacques Cousteau titles among his books and the mere mention of them proved the key to opening up an area of Fleming's life that I had not heard or read about before.

'I have always been fascinated with treasure hunting,' he said, drawing on his cigarette and exhaling the smoke through his nostrils. 'I used to go looking for buried treasure when I was a child and it still interests me today. It has popped up regularly during my life and so far I've used the idea in two of the Bond books, *Live and Let Die* (1954) and the latest, *On Her Majesty's Secret Service*.' Fleming's eyes glinted as he recalled for me the childhood incident with the 'ambergris', his encounter with the fabulous crown jewels of Albania and the 'treasure hunts' for German secret documents during the war.

His first experience of a real treasure hunt had taken place in April 1953 just after the publication of *Casino Royale*. He was sent by the *Sunday Times* to Marseilles where Jacques Cousteau was exploring the wreck of a Graeco-Roman galley which had sunk in a storm in 250 BC just off the island of Grand Congloue. The vessel had been preserved in a thick layer of mud and Fleming was offered the chance of going down with the underwater explorer to watch the salvage work.

During the next two weeks, the former commander made several dives from the Frenchman's ship, the *Calypso*, relishing the opportunity to see the items of centuries-old treasure being discovered in the wreck and hauled to the surface. Later he wrote in the *Sunday Times*, 'I cannot describe the romance and excitement of the scene better than to say that it contained at the same time elements from *King Solomon's Mines*, *Treasure Island* and *The Swiss Family Robinson*.' For a time after this, Fleming nursed a dream of forgetting all about writing fiction and concentrating on becoming *the* journalist of the underwater world. Instead, though, he put the experience to more immediate use in *Live and Let Die* on which he was then working.

In this second James Bond adventure, Fleming describes a not dissimilar underwater treasure hunt for the lost ship of the seventeenth-century British buccaneer, Sir Henry Morgan, who turned around his life of villainy on the high seas to become lieutenant-governor of Jamaica. To ensure that he got the details of the hoard right, Fleming went to Spink's of St James's, dealers in rare coins, to find out about the silver pieces of eight and various seventeenth-century gold coins which Mr Big, the criminal mastermind behind the operation, uses to finance his criminal network on behalf of SMERSH.

Fleming utilised the sensations he had enjoyed off the coast of France to give added authenticity to 007's underwater swim to Mr Big's ship, the *Secatur*, to fix a limpet mine to the hull. And when he returned to Goldeneye that winter, the waters around the coast became an even greater magnet to him for snorkelling and exploration.

At the end of his article about the Cousteau explorations, Fleming had appealed to readers of the *Sunday Times* to send in any tales of buried treasure they might have come across. Hundreds of letters poured into the newspaper's offices and he spent days reading them, sorting out those that had enough validity to make them worth pursuing.

'I looked into the practicalities of treasure hunting,' he recalled, lighting another cigarette. 'I met an inspector of the Special Branch at Scotland Yard who gave me some tips about the kind of places people hid money and valuables. I talked to one of the experts at the deep-sea diving company, Siebe Gorman, about the problems of finding underwater treasure and I even went to the Royal Engineers to get the latest gen on the methods of mine detection. They even promised me some Sappers to help in any search I undertook!'

Gradually, Fleming narrowed down the choice from sunken galleons in the English Channel and Viking relics in the Cambridgeshire Fens, to Creake Abbey near Burnham Market in Norfolk where a huge cache of silver and gold was supposed to have been buried by the monks to prevent it being seized by Henry VIII's assessors. He took up the Royal Engineers' offer and, accompanied by three Sappers, spent three days methodically covering every inch of the old abbey from the cloisters to the ancient chapter house. In the end, even the patience of a lifelong treasure hunter became exhausted and Fleming was forced to write ruefully: 'In two days we dug up about thirty nails of different sizes, one frying pan, one mole trap, one oil drum and about a hundredweight of miscellaneous scrap iron. Our jokes about twelfth-century sardine tins ceased at an early stage.'

Although the failure of the treasure hunt provided nothing directly for the Bond saga, one letter that Fleming read stuck in his mind and he made use of it in the series almost ten years later.

'It was about a hoard of gold that was apparently on its way from North Africa to Berlin in 1942 when the ship carrying it was sunk,' Fleming told me. 'The rumours said it was loot that Rommel had collected in North Africa and was sending back to Hitler as a present. The vessel sank somewhere off the coast of Corsica. I thought it would make a good story, but it would have taken more money than the *Sunday Times* could afford. The paper was going through a hard time then, so I did not even bother to suggest it.'

As he had done so often before, though, Fleming made good use of the information. He saved the story of Rommel's Gold until he wrote *On Her Majesty's Secret Service* in 1963 – the book I had come to talk to him about prior to its publication in paperback. In it, Bond sets out to thwart the plans of Ernst Stavro Blofeld and SPECTRE to overwhelm Britain by waging biological warfare on the nation's agriculture.

Noting my interest, Fleming directed me to the pages where 007 has just met Marc-Ange Draco, the engaging and benevolent Corsican-born *Capu* of the Union Corse which controls organised crime throughout France and her colonies, and is recalling some of the tales associated with the deadly organisation. Bond thinks in particular about the 'mysterious business of Rommel's treasure' which is supposed to lie hidden beneath the sea somewhere off Bastia. He knows that in 1948, a Czech diver called Fleigh was supposed to have been on the track of the fortune, but was warned off by the Union and promptly vanished.

More recently, Bond knows, the body of a young French diver, André Mattei, was found ridded with bullets. The man had been boasting in the local bars that he knew the whereabouts of the treasure and had come to dive for it. He paid for his foolishness with his life.

At first glance, the stories seemed like pure fiction, added to give more excitement and the threat of danger to James Bond's latest exploit. But I had already come to appreciate during our talk just how well founded Ian Fleming's stories were in fact and the hooded eyes that stared across the desk at me as I looked up from reading the book were unmistakably direct even through the veil of cigarette smoke.

Fleming clearly believed there was something in the legend and I had no reason to disagree. I knew his career in Intelligence had taken him to the very heart of the story in North Africa and this was just one of many reasons that came into my head – then and later – to explain why the story should have so captured his interest.

The pursuit of gold was, clearly, more than just a fantasy to Fleming: it can be seen as a recurring theme in his work. Take *Goldfinger* (1959), about the SMERSH conspiracy to steal all the gold in Fort Knox. For this Bond adventure Fleming took the trouble to obtain first-hand information from a leading

London goldsmith, Guy Wellby about the smelting, transporting and smuggling of the precious metal. In the short story *Octopussy*, written in 1962 but not published until after the author's death, Bond wrings the location of a hidden hoard of Nazi gold from a former British wartime commando who then allows himself to be stung to death by a poisonous scorpion fish.

Following the success of the first series of *Sunday Times* articles about treasure hunting, Fleming wrote the outline for a play in which a treasure hunter finds gold and is able to 'cock a snook at authority and have everything his own way'. And in 1958, still on treasure hunts for the *Sunday Times*, he visited the beautiful Seychelles in the Indian Ocean in an unsuccessful search for a hoard of gold doubloons, said to be worth over £120,000, which had been buried on the island of Mahé by the eigthteenth-century French pirate, Olivier Le Vasseur.

Fleming's enduring interest was also captivated by the tale of a German ship, the *Koenigsberg*, which had been carrying a cache of fabulous riches when it was sunk near the same islands during the First World War. Both of these stories were featured in his subsequent article, 'Treasure Hunt in Eden' which, if it did nothing to satisfy his yen for finding lost hoards, did a great deal to stimulate tourist interest in the remote Seychelles.

Our conversation that day in the office in Mitre Court ended after Fleming's revelation about Rommel's Gold. Almost immediately afterwards, he asked to be excused as he was due to meet a friend for a drink in the famous Fleet Street wine bar, El Vino's, just across the courtyard. For my part, my head was still buzzing with everything he had told me and I went back to my own office at Ludgate Circus to start work on my article.

Sadly, I never met Ian Fleming again – he died, aged just 56, less than a year later on 11 August 1964, disregarding to the end his doctor's instructions to cut down on his smoking and drinking – but my interview with him remains one of the most memorable of my journalistic career.

Indeed, from that day the story of Rommel's Gold began to haunt me. For some years other projects kept me fully occupied, but the legend of the extraordinary hoard would surface in my mind from time to time just as it must have done for Ian Fleming. Finally, I resolved to do something about it – as I like to imagine that dedicated treasure hunter himself would have done, given the time and opportunity.

But before I could even begin to look for a solution to the mystery, I knew I would have to make a study of the life and career of the man after whom the gold was named, in order to discover precisely what was his involvement – a man who had left his name for ever associated with one of the crucial battles of the Second World War.

3

The Cunning of The Desert Fox

Field Marshal Erwin Rommel, the commander of the German Afrika Korps, was nicknamed 'The Desert Fox' because of his extraordinary skill at waging war in the blistering wastes of North Africa. He used speed, surprise, daring and, particularly, deception against the British forces, to seize over 1,500 miles of territory from Tunisia through Libya to the border of Egypt. Like the animal with which he was compared, Rommel was cunning, quick-thinking and merciless, both militarily and by nature – and when the facts of his life and career are examined it seems somehow appropriate that the most famous lost hoard of treasure from the Second World War should be named after him.

It is evident that from the outset of his operations in North Africa, Rommel liked to be in the thick of the fighting, leading his men from the very front of the action. Indeed, he often raced ahead of his troops with characteristic audacity and not surprisingly often came under fire from all and sundry – British, Italian and even, occasionally, German guns. He had a capacity, almost a wish, to expose himself to personal danger – and an equal amount of good fortune to escape it.

Rommel was a fast mover and a master of *Blitzkrieg*, once summing up his philosophy in these words: 'I took risks against all orders and instructions because the opportunity seemed favourable.'

He always dressed immaculately, too, despite the carnage of war and the intense heat of the desert; his Iron Cross hung visibly at his throat, presenting the same image of dash and insouciance as a cavalry officer in the American Civil War. Small wonder that Hitler came to hold Rommel in the highest regard – 'His mere name suddenly begins to acquire the value of several divisions,' the Führer is reported to have said during a dinner-table conversation with other German officers in 1942 – and a legend grew around him, both among his own troops and those of the enemy.

By March 1942, General Sir Claude Auchinleck, the British commander in North Africa, had become extremely concerned about what was perceived as the almost magical skills of his opponent. 'We have to get this stinker down where he belongs,' he told a member of his staff and issued a directive about Rommel to all his commanders and chiefs-of-staff that is surely unique in the annals of the Second World War:

> There exists a danger that our friend Rommel is becoming a kind of bogey-man to our troops, who are talking too much about him. He is by no means a superman, although he is very energetic and able. Even if he were a superman, it would still be highly undesirable that our men should credit him with supernatural powers.
>
> I wish you to dispel by all possible means the idea that Rommel represents something more than an ordinary German general. The important thing now is to see to it that

we do not always talk of Rommel when we mean the enemy in Libya. We must refer to 'the Germans' or 'the Axis powers' or 'the enemy' and not always keep harping on Rommel. Please ensure that this order is put into immediate effect and impress upon all Commanders that, from a psychological point of view, it is a matter of the highest importance.

Yet, despite this assurance by Auchinleck – which probably only enhanced Rommel's stature, as such statements have a habit of doing – there undoubtedly *was* something very out of the ordinary about this fair-haired German soldier whose sharp blue eyes hinted at hidden cunning. He was, in truth, a man who had learned all about the advantages of being deceptive and crafty right from the days of his childhood.

Johannes Erwin Rommel was born on 15 November 1891 at Heidenheim in the state of Württemberg, the second son of an autocratic maths teacher. He was a small, pale, sickly child with a sneaky cleverness and a calculating grin that would mark him out for the rest of his life.

As a teenager he appears to have been interested in engineering and with a friend, Hans Keitel, actually built a small box-type glider, although there is no evidence that it ever flew more than a few yards. Rommel senior, however, had ambitions for his son to join the Army and in March 1911 helped him to gain entry to the Officers' Military School in Danzig.

Despite his small stature, young Rommel proved an enthusiastic and dedicated soldier. On the outbreak of the First World War, he served with the 124th Infantry, mainly in France. Here he showed great bravery in trench warfare as well as a natural bent for leadership and, following his appointment as a lieutenant in 1915, led a daring raid on four French bunkers which earned him an Iron Cross.

Some of Rommel's biographers believe he earned his nickname at this juncture of his career, long before he went to Africa. They cite as evidence a photograph taken of the young lieutenant at the front posing with a tame fox at his side.

A later posting to Italy as the commander of an *Abteilung* (detachment) saw Rommel demonstrating the use of speed, surprise, bluff and courage to outwit often larger companies of the enemy in the mountain ranges of the Julian Alps. In this rocky, snowy terrain the ambitious young soldier began to hone the tactical ability that he would later use with such devastating effect in North Africa. He had become, in the words of Brigadier Desmond Young in *Rommel* (1950), 'the perfect fighting animal'.

By the end of the war in 1918, Rommel had obtained the rank of captain. In the interim he had married Lucie, also a schoolmaster's child, with whom he would have a son, Manfred. Thanks to the terms of the Armistice between the combatants, the German Army remained intact and Rommel was able to continue as an instructor in the sole occupation for which he was ideally suited.

In 1937, he drew on his hard-won experience of combat and work as an instructor at the Potsdam school of infantry to write *Infanterie Greift An (The Infantry Attacks)*, complete with his own illustrations. It became an immediate best-seller.

The book's vivid narrative of hand-to-hand fighting and methods of outwitting the enemy and killing him – as well as its innovative approach to military techniques – appealed to soldiers and civilians alike, especially the new generation of restless young men. The book's success also brought him a small fortune – with all the attendant problems of sudden wealth.

However, Rommel's cunning instincts enabled him to outwit the German income tax authorities when the time came to make his annual returns, according to David Irving in *The Trail of the Fox*. Instead of taking lump sums, he instructed his publishers to pay him just 15,000 Reichmarks per year and place the rest in a bank deposit to earn interest. He then declared the much-reduced figure and avoided heavy taxes. For the rest of his life, Rommel would use similar techniques to conceal his real wealth.

The success of *Infanterie Greift An* may have escaped the attention of the taxman, but it did bring him to the attention of someone else with whom his destiny would become linked: Adolf Hitler. The Nazi Party had, of course, come to power in 1933 with promises to solve unemployment and restore national pride and military strength. Their leader could hardly fail to have been aware of the best-selling manual and, with his passion for military information, certainly read it. There is no doubt, either, that Rommel was a great admirer of the man who promised a new era for Germany, as historian David Fraser has written in *Knight's Cross*:

For himself, Rommel admired Hitler unreservedly. He had always been grateful for what, as he reckoned, Hitler had so far done for Germany. He had been comforted by the immense restoration of national morale Hitler had brought about. He had marvelled at what seemed the diplomatic skill by which Hitler had achieved so many patriotic ends with so little international opposition; and he had turned his attention away from the excesses, the blemishes, as things typical of some of the undesirables who had always attached themselves to Hitler, but utterly untypical of the Führer himself. With Hitler, Rommel's relations became easy, friendly, gratifying and he had frequent chats with him.

Hitler, in turn, sensed the potential of the soldier-writer. In late August 1939, Rommel was summoned to Berlin to become *Kommandant* of the Führer's headquarters as the attack on Poland was set in motion – and, with it, the outbreak of the Second World War. After being installed in his office in the Reich Chancellery, Rommel confessed in a letter to his wife, Lucie, that the trust that Hitler placed in him meant more than the promotion itself.

The sudden success of the Polish campaign and Hitler's evident intention to extend the boundaries of Germany elsewhere made Rommel yearn to be back in action. He used the fact that he now had personal access to the dictator to ask for the command of an armoured division of the Wehrmacht. He fancied one of the vaunted Panzer divisions and although it was pointed out to Hitler by several of his senior military commanders that Rommel had no experience of tanks, the Führer overruled their objections and agreed to his request. In February 1940, Rommel was put in charge of the 7th Panzer Division earmarked for the invasion of France.

Before leaving to take up his new posting, Rommel dined with Hitler once more. As the two men parted, Hitler handed over a copy of his own best-seller, *Mein Kampf*, inscribed 'To General Rommel with pleasant memories'. It was a gift that

Rommel vowed to repay in actions, deeds or in any other way that might please his leader.

Newly appointed as a general Rommel may have been – and an infantryman by training – he took with great facility to the role of tank commander. He appreciated, cleverly, that handling armoured, mobile forces did not owe everything to a specialised knowledge of technology as some might claim – although he had always displayed a facility with machinery since his teenage years tinkering with the glider. It was also necessary to understand the shifting but essentially unchanging principles of war.

Rommel gave full attention to learning all about the massive, twenty-ton Panzer III and IV tanks under his command. With their 320hp Maybach petrol engines capable of speeds of up to 25mph, the nine-foot-tall monsters were capable of wreaking terrible damage upon other machines, all but the strongest buildings and particularly on the enemy. They were almost impervious to gunfire, though they seemed like hell on wheels for the crew of five lurching and sweating in the cramped interior.

History records that Rommel's 7th Division carried out the tactics of *Blitzkrieg* with devastating effect across Belgium and France right up to the English Channel, albeit that the opposition was limited. The speed of their arrival caught many of the defending troops unprepared and thousands were taken prisoner almost before they had time to fire a single shot.

Time and again Rommel put himself in danger of sniper fire as he rode at the front of his advancing Panzers in the turret of his tank, immaculately dressed and with his medals gleaming. But his luck, not to mention his cunning, held good. He was, as Charles Douglas-Home writes in *Rommel*, 'a man possessed, sustained almost to addiction by the adrenalin of war'.

When news of Rommel's success reached Hitler's ears, the General became the first divisional commander in France to be awarded a Knight's Cross – an honour which further cemented his admiration for the Führer. By the time he reached Cherbourg, Rommel had more to boast about than a medal, as he later confided in a letter to Lucie: 'Only by striking fast have we been able to execute the Führer's specific order that Cherbourg was to be captured as rapidly as possible... I've slept seven hours now, and I'm going out to look over my troops, our prisoners and the *immense booty*.'

The seizing of the spoils of war was, of course, commonplace among troops of all nationalities during the Second World War. Ordinary German and British soldiers, as well as their officers and commanders, helped themselves to any weapons, foodstuffs or clothing that the retreating enemy had not taken the trouble – or been allowed the time – to retrieve or destroy.

In many cases, too, the abandoned homes of the civilian population were looted and hardly a day passed without more valuable paintings, artefacts and furnishings being dispatched from French cities and towns back to Germany for the growing collections of the leaders of the Third Reich.

There is, however, no record of Rommel's intentions, honourable or otherwise, about the destiny of the booty he found in Cherbourg. Certainly, it is the first indication we have that he was interested in the spoils of war and might covet them, for whatever reason. In all probability, though, he was still high on the adrenalin of his all-conquering military operation and the acknowledgement its success had merited from Hitler.

In fact the seizure of war treasure would not become associated with the name of Rommel – or form a part of his legend – until his next posting: far away from the grey seas of the English Channel on the exotic Mediterranean shoreline of North Africa.

Rommel spent the summer of 1940 fretting on the coast of France, hoping for an invasion of England that never came. Even an invitation to the Reich Chancellery in September turned out only to be a meeting between Hitler and his generals to discuss the general state of the war. During his time in Berlin, though, Rommel was undoubtedly flattered to find his exploits pictured in many magazines and featured in a film, *Victory in the West*, which had been made by the Nazi Propaganda Minister, Josef Goebbels – never one to miss the chance of exploiting a public hero.

It is possible that at this time Rommel nursed the hope of being given a command on the Eastern Front when the attack on Russia, code-named 'Barbarossa', was put into effect. Instead, when the grandiloquent Italian dictator Benito Mussolini's plans for taking Egypt and the Suez Canal from the British foundered in the winter of 1940, the Führer offered reinforcements in the shape of two tank divisions. He had just the man to take charge of the job, too.

So, resplendent with the title of *Oberbefehlshaber* (Commander-in-Chief) Afrika Korps, Erwin Rommel found himself on the morning of 12 February 1941 arriving at the port of Tripoli in Libya to face a completely new challenge with his tanks in the desert wastes of North Africa.

It was a challenge to relish, too – and his appointment proved a masterstroke. Free of the shackles of a larger operation like that in France and fellow commanders who constantly argued over his strategy, Rommel had a free hand to activate an amended version of the *Blitzkrieg* tactics that he so favoured. The results were staggering.

Within weeks of his arrival with 20,000 troops and orders to galvanise the struggling Italians, he had forced the British back 600 miles across the Libyan desert, transforming a holding action into a drive that soon threatened the Suez Canal. Elated accounts in the German media of the time speak of Rommel's 'artful smile' as he sped across the desert, the 'cunning look in his clear blue eyes' evident as one objective after another was achieved. Small wonder that he was soon being referred to everywhere by the soubriquet of 'The Desert Fox'.

Rommel employed every cunning idea he could think of to deceive and outwit the enemy. He arranged for tanks newly arrived in Tripoli to be driven around the streets several times in order to confuse any enemy agents who might be watching as to their numerical strength. He had brooms and rags attached to the back of all military vehicles so as to stir up the dust and give the impression of a huge army approaching. And he enhanced his own aura of invincibility by heading the chase across the fiery inferno of the desert sands.

The British forces under General Auchinleck were undoubtedly surprised by Rommel's adroitness after the ineffectiveness of the Italians. By the end of 1941, although the German tanks had been checked to some degree by the stubborn resistance of the British forces – and in particular by the Australians at Ras el Mdauuar – 'The Desert Fox' unquestionably held the upper hand. As he crossed Cyrenaica with Tobruk and the borders of Egypt in his sights, his stature as an icon was growing daily.

The Commander-in-Chief had taken to travelling in a new form of transport: a large armoured truck the size of a small bus that ran on oversized tyres and was ideal for all forms of desert travel. Known as the *Mammut* ('mammoth') it was actually a British armoured command vehicle that had been captured along with other military booty at Mechili as Auchinleck's troops retreated across Cyrenaica. Charles Douglas-Home records that as soon as Rommel clapped eyes on the vehicle he climbed aboard and declared to his men, 'Booty! – permissible, I take it, even for a general!'

The sides of the vehicle were still painted in their original blue and grey camouflage, with the addition of a Wehrmacht cross on the front and rear. The driver's windshield was made of armoured glass and there was a small hatch just behind the co-driver's seat through which Rommel could thrust his head and shoulders to survey the surrounding terrain. The *Mammut*, too, soon became part of the legend.

Rommel added a new element to his own image – a pair of large Perspex goggles, also purloined at Machili. Whether worn over his eyes or perched on the peak of his cap, these glasses, glinting in the harsh desert sunlight, soon became instantly recognisable to his men even when he was some distance away. As one of his old friends, General Ulrich de Maiziere, remarked later, according to Desmond Young, 'He deliberately played the part with his clothes. He wore goggles and a leather greatcoat, with his medals always visible and his cap at a jaunty angle.'

Although often unhappy at the efforts of Mussolini's troops, Rommel continued to battle his way across Libya. On 15 January 1942, nine merchant ships docked at Tripoli bringing him much-needed supplies of provisions and fuel as well as fifty new tanks.

A fortnight later, on 28 January, he once again used his mastery of surprise and deception to attack Benghazi, looting all the equipment and stores he could find – including urgently needed trucks and crates of canned meat, butter, preserves, fruit, chocolate, beer and cigarettes – before disappearing back into the desert with goodies for his delighted troops.

Then, in May, with a force that consisted of considerably fewer tanks than Auchinleck's, Rommel defeated the British at Gazala – a great achievement in anybody's estimation. Hitler was quick to congratulate him – 'Tell Rommel that I admire him' – and awarded him the Swords to his Knight's Cross. At once Rommel began to plan the glittering prize he would offer in return to his Führer – the Allied forces' mighty stronghold of Tobruk near the Egyptian border. He set a date of 26 May for the start of the attack by a combination of 550 Afrika Korps and Italian tanks.

The battle proved costly to Rommel in terms of both men and machinery, however. Intense heat and sandstorms delayed his advance, as did the heroic resistance of the Allied troops in the now encircled stronghold. Attacks by German fighter planes and bombers continued relentlessly as the *Oberbefehlshaber* organised a number of diversionary operations on the Egyptian side of Tobruk to deceive the beleaguered troops.

On 20 June, after almost a month of intense conflict, Rommel   *X* stormed into the city. At once he telegraphed Berlin: 'My troops have crowned their efforts by the capture of Tobruk.'

Immediately on taking control of the city and accepting the surrender of the South African Commandant, General Klopper, Rommel insisted that all tanks and trucks had to be handed over undamaged. Installing himself in a former hotel, the Albergo Tobruk, he began to take stock of the 'treasure troves of Tobruk' as Brigadier Desmond Young has described the situation in which the victor found himself.

Apart from the captured weapons and ammunition, there were warehouses stuffed with clothing, provisions, beer and cigarettes that seemed like manna from heaven to the exhausted tank crews. But it was the loot – in the form of gold bullion and currency – that had fallen into the victors' hands that undoubtedly excited most interest among the officers.

Back in Berlin, after the news of the taking of Tobruk had been relayed by the media, Hitler was quick to reward the man whose name was now a household word – promoting Rommel to the rank of *Generalfeldmarschall*. It was the highest honour any German soldier could attain, one he would hold for life and which would entitle him to a string of luxuries. It also put Rommel above dismissal and gave him almost limitless authority.

But in Africa, Rommel was determined not to rest on his laurels. His ambition had always been to seize Egypt and the Suez Canal and on 23 June he began making plans to push on with his Panzer Army towards the next British stronghold, the important naval base at Alexandria, just over 100 miles away. However, the unexpected appearance of RAF bombers overhead the very next day clearly indicated that although the British might have lost one city, the battle for North Africa was far from over.

The truth was that the tide was about to turn against Rommel. Allied reinforcements were starting to arrive in greater numbers thanks to Winston Churchill's insistence on the vital importance of the British presence in the Mediterranean.

Unexpectedly – certainly unforeseen by Rommel – the German advance was halted at El Alamein. Here he was compelled to face the fact that the Afrika Korps were being inhibited in their progress because the supply and communication lines stretching back to Tripoli were now overextended and could not keep pace with his demands for fuel and amunition.

Then, in August, the man who would prove to be Rommel's nemesis arrived in Africa – British Lieutenant-General Bernard Montgomery, who had been sent to replace Auchinleck. A professional soldier to the core, like his adversary he was small and cunning, with a similar predeliction for publicity. Likewise something of an eccentric, he wore an Australian bush hat covered with medals. Montgomery sensed the challenge of a lifetime in hounding the forces of The Desert Fox to destruction.

Rommel's defeat at El Alamein in October 1942 – in a battle which began with the biggest artillery barrage by British Army troops since 1914–18 – is one of the defining moments of the Second World War. As Winston Churchill was to put it later, 'Before Alamein we never had a victory – after Alamein we never had a defeat.'

The *Generalfeldmarschall* suffered massive casualties and the destruction of 260 German and Italian tanks as Montgomery pulled the Afrika Korps around the battlefield this way and that with one brilliant tactical move after another. The cunning German had met his match in the equally crafty Englishman and by the conclusion over 9,000 prisoners had been taken.

In September Rommel, bone-tired and ill, was granted leave and flew back to Germany to his wife and son. He was replaced by General Georg Stumme, an expert in Panzer warfare, whose orders were to hold the positions Rommel had established and augment them with minefields nicknamed 'Devil's Gardens'. Tragically, Rommel had scarcely begun to enjoy his much-needed break when on 25 October Stumme suffered a heart attack and died, and the Field Marshal was ordered back to Libya.

By early November, despite Rommel's best efforts at sitting tight, Montgomery had forced him into retreat. This was completely contrary to Hitler's express orders to stand firm – 'You must show your troops no other road but victory or death,' the Führer had cabled him – and from now on the dictator would become increasingly disillusioned with his one-time all-conquering hero.

The Desert Fox was now seriously outnumbered by the British, both in terms of men and equipment, and on 4 November he began what would prove to be a painful odyssey of hardship and death for him and his remaining 7,500 German and Italian troops as they retreated 2,000 miles back to their starting point in Tripoli.

Throughout this period, though, Rommel employed every ounce of his old cunning to keep out of range of the deadly fire of his pursuers, avoid the traps set for his sixty-mile-long procession of vehicles, and make the most of his fast declining supplies of fuel, ammunition and provisions. Some military historians have described the retreat as a masterpiece of tactics that saved countless lives, but there is no denying the whole exercise was a bitter pill for the *Generalfeldmarschall* to swallow. He wrote in a letter to his wife, 'The dead are lucky – it's all over for them.'

Reaching the safety of Tunisia in May 1943, Rommel did not have to wait long before he was summoned back to Germany by Hitler and spared having to witness the final collapse of the remaining Afrika Korps force that he had once made seem invincible throughout North Africa. The Desert Fox was now history and his exploits – both those on record and others that would form his legend – were beginning to shift one way and another like the sands of Africa where they had taken place.

The rest of Field Marshal Erwin Rommel's anticlimactic career is simply told. Once back in Germany again, it did not take him long to sum up the situation and realise that all was not going well with the war. Although clearly unsettled by this, he accepted the command of Army Group B in France, which was expected to defend the country from an anticipated Allied invasion. Here, though, he soon clashed over tactics with his superior, Field Marshal Gerd von Rundstedt, although both were agreed on the inherent weaknesses of the much-vaunted armoured 'Atlantic Wall' stretching along the coastline of Occupied Europe facing England and urged Hitler to order more fortifications before it was too late. On 6 June 1944 – D-Day – their worst fears were confirmed.

Just over a month later, on 17 July, Rommel's staff car was strafed by an RAF Spitfire near Berney and his injuries necessitated his hospitalisation in Paris. While he was recuperating, the attempted assassination of Hitler by a group of his officers took place on 20 July and shortly afterwards a startled Rommel found himself implicated. It transpired that during the investigation by Gestapo officers into the conspiracy, his name had been heard whispered by several of the plotters.

When Rommel, too, was closely cross-questioned it was apparent just how far his stock had slumped. For once there was nothing the crafty old fox could do to extricate himself – although it seems abundantly clear he knew nothing whatsoever about the plot.

The once untouchable national hero now found himself being offered the alternatives of a trial for treason or suicide. He was told that the Führer himself had promised that if he chose the latter his reputation would be safe and his family would be spared from humiliation. There would be a state funeral and a monument would be erected to his memory. Was this, Rommel may have wondered to himself, intended as a last gift from the man to whom he had given so much?

On the morning of 14 October, the old soldier sat in the back of his car and took a sip from a cyanide ampoule. His heart stopped almost immediately. Later that day, an official announcement informed the German people that Field Marshal Erwin Rommel had died as a result of the injuries sustained in the RAF attack. The man who had been described by Churchill as 'a very daring and skilful opponent' and a battlefield leader of genius was no more.

It would not be until after the end of the war that the facts about Rommel's death would become generally known: although long before then his legend was securely enshrined in the history of the war.

But how did his name become linked to a fabulous lost hoard of gold and where had this treasure come from? To find the answers to these questions we need to go back to the very start of the German occupation of North Africa and a time of persecution and terror in the exotic country of Tunisia.

4

The Price of Freedom

Tunisia is one of the smallest countries in North Africa, fronting on to the Mediterranean and sandwiched between Algeria to the west and Libya to the east. Covering just over 48,000 square miles, it is about the same size as England, its terrain varying from well-forested mountains and fertile plains in the north to the Shott el Jerid salt lakes and a great swathe of the Sahara desert in the south.

The nation has endured a chequered history. First settled by Phoenician merchants in the eleventh century BC, it passed through the hands of the Greeks, Romans and Turks before the French took the country by force in 1881. Despite the emergence of nationalism in 1920 through the efforts of the *Destour* (Constitutional) Party, followed by the slaughter of 122 protesters in front of the French Residence on 9 April 1938 – a day which has gone down in local history as the 'Martyrs' Day' – Tunisia was still firmly a French protectorate when the Second World War broke out.

After the fall of France and the armistice agreed with Germany by Marshal Pétain's Vichy government in June 1940 – plus the subsequent Italian entry into the war – the implications for Tunisia and its mixed population of 2,600,000 soon became apparent. Apart from the two million Muslims living in the country, there were also just over 108,000 French, 94,000 Italians and some 60,000 Jews.

Even before the arrival of Axis troops, the Jewish population had reason to be fearful about their future. For years until the middle of the nineteenth century, they had been isolated from the Muslims who despised them and forced them to live in separate quarters. Then, in 1859, the anti-Semitic laws had been abolished, enabling the Jewish people to use their skills, powers of adaptation and practical abilities to good effect – although not always without attracting envy and even outright hostility.

The Jews who had originated from Italy – known as Leghorn Jews – had in the main become bankers, money-lenders, traders and businessmen; while the poorer indigenous Jews who dressed like natives tended to follow the professions of tailors, shoemakers, butchers and small shopkeepers. By 1940, the main colonies were to be found in the capital, Tunis, as well as Bizerte, La Goulette, Nabeul, Sousse, Sfax, Gabès and the Ile de Djerba.

Accounts written at the time indicate that most of the Jewish population were pro-French, although they felt strongly that they should be granted citizenship en bloc as had happened in Algeria, where all Jews had been naturalised by a decree of 1870. A special report prepared in 1942 by the British Naval Intelligence Division under the instructions of Admiral John Godfrey (Ian Fleming's boss), *B.R. 523 Tunisia*, marked 'Restricted: For Official Use Only' and intended for Army, Navy and RAF commanders, put the situation in which this section of the population found themselves in no uncertain terms:

Since 1930, anti-Jewish feeling among the Moslems has been stirred up by the Italians in Tunisia, and between 1931 and 1933 there were riots against the Jews, which led to the suppression of the *Destour* party responsible for the outbreaks. After the armistice in 1940, the Vichy government adopted an anti-Jewish policy, the basic anti-Jewish statute of metropolitan France being extended, with certain modifications, to Tunisian Jews by Beylical decree on 4 December 1940.

It was evident from this statement that the Jewish population of Tunisia could expect little support or protection from either the government or the other ethnic groups when those infamous anti-Semites, the Nazis, began arriving in 1941 to support the Italian campaign of conquest in North Africa. Indeed, Albert Memmi, the Tunisian writer who was born the son of a leather worker in the Jewish ghetto of Tunis and spent much of the occupation in a forced work camp, has described the immediate impact of the German arrival with chilling effect:

The morning after the German Junkers started landing, the German *Kommandatur*, armed with very accurate lists, took several hundred hostages. Then the demands and killings began. The German soldiers took pot shots into windows, pillaged and raped. Night-time bombardments disorientated people further.

The Jews realised precisely how alone they were and some tried to leave the country. Eight days after their arrival, the Germans began rounding up Jewish men between 18 to 40 to take them to work camps. The Jewish appeal to the *Résidence Générale* [J P Esteva] met with a reply that he was under the orders of the Germans. In a sentence, France was abandoning the Jews.

The next two years were to be a nightmare for Tunisia's Jewish population, a time of persecution, terror and death on an everyday basis. It that would only end with the Allied invasion of the country – and not before a deal had been struck that would result in the collection of a multi-million-pound treasure trove subsequently named after the most famous German general in North Africa.

In the interim, that man, Field Marshal Rommel, had crossed Libya to the very borders of Egypt and been driven back, defeated, to Tunisia, leaving along the way the clues that would begin the association of his name with the fabulous hoard.

It was not, in fact, until after the war was over that it became evident *how* Rommel's Gold had earned its name. The facts revealed both how the link had been formed and how the rumours of its existence had arisen, creating a story as strange as any in mystery fiction.

Aside from the valuable paintings and objets d'art that we know were being gathered especially for Hitler's Führermuseum, the war was a constant drain on the German economy and any means of bolstering the treasury were encouraged. The evidence shows that hoards of cash and valuables flowed in a constant stream back to the Reich as her conquering armies spread across Europe and Russia and on to the African continent.

It is against the background of these well-known activities that rumours started about the triumphant Rommel dispatching to

Germany a priceless collection of the spoils of war from North Africa. What seemed indisputable, however, was that this loot never arrived. But if, as these stories claimed, Rommel *had* come into possession of a great treasure, where had it come from, how could it have been transported, and if so, by whom?

The answer to the first question would seem to be obviously Libya. In the previous chapter I have detailed the Field Marshal's triumphs and the several occasions on which he refers to the loot that has fallen into his hands – especially the 'treasure troves of Tobruk' where he could certainly have assembled a king's ransom to present as a gift to Hitler or the Reich Chancellery.

Again, it is not difficult to find an answer for the second question. The ideal form of transport for any spoils would surely have been Rommel's command vehicle, the giant *Mammut*, which had space enough in the interior for half a dozen cases. Indeed, one rumour insists there was a custom-built locker over the driving shaft of the ACV which the Field Marshal had specially installed.

And as to transporting the treasure out of North Africa there were two options: by air on one of the many Luftwaffe aircraft that flew from Libya to Italy and Germany; or, alternately, on one of the numerous ships making the round trip with ammunition, fuel and provisions for the Afrika Korps.

Virtually until the end of the war in North Africa, flights in and out of the battle zone took place on an almost daily basis, transporting senior military personnel backwards and forwards. The checking of the identity papers of these men was cursory at best and their cases, bags and packages were mostly emblazoned with the words *GEHEIM!* (Top Secret) or *VERSCHLUSSSACHE* (Classified).

Merchant ships, too, crossed and re-crossed the Mediterranean: some from Germany, many more from nearby Italy. The supremacy of the U-boats in the region made their passage, in general, secure – until, that is, the British seizure of the German Enigma code machine which provided the Allies with the capability to decipher their enemies' messages.

As to who might have *personally* carried out the transportation, there are two prime suspects, if we are to believe the rumours. Rommel himself would clearly not have the time for any such task, constantly preoccupied as he was with the war. But he did have two trusted officers, Lieutenant Alfred Berndt and Corporal Albert Böttcher, who had both the time and the opportunity. The two men were, it seems, selflessly devoted to the Field Marshal and the Führer.

Alfred Berndt was an officer from Josef Goebbels's Propaganda Ministry who had been seconded to Rommel's staff as his chief aide when the *Generalfeldmarschall* was assigned to North Africa. Goebbels was, of course, well aware of the advantages of having someone on the spot to report The Desert Fox's triumphs and there is no doubt that Berndt played a crucial part in the creation of the Rommel legend.

A rugged, 36-year-old Berliner, Berndt had a reputation for being forthright and determined. He was also clever and adept at dealing with military personnel, and he quickly developed a rapport with Rommel. The Field Marshal had long been given to speaking his mind and indications are that the two men shared many intimacies as the tank war took them headlong across Libya.

Lieutenant Berndt's primary function was to keep Rommel's diary as well as making regular propaganda broadcasts to

Germany. He famously declared on one occasion of his chief, 'He is a master of deception and disguises and always does what one least expects.'

It is evident that Berndt ran errands and was not averse to tackling the occasional tough assignment or doing the odd dirty chore. Indeed, it is clear from entries in the diary that he was several times sent by Rommel to see Hitler and inform him of specific problems being experienced in the war. Sometimes Berndt was even called upon to perform such intimate tasks as writing Rommel's letters to his wife, Lucie.

The Field Marshal, for his part, was always keen to take the Lieutenant along on his more audacious manoeuvres in the desert. On one night reconnaissance drive across the border into Egypt, their vehicle broke down in the sand and they had a lucky escape when they were rescued by the all-purpose *Mammut*. Unlike many of Rommel's other achievements, this unnerving experience was not considered suitable for any of Berndt's radio dispatches to Berlin. He did, though, provide a vivid eyewitness account of Rommel's capture of Tobruk which earned record listening figures when it was broadcast back home.

According to the rumours, Berndt took several trips to Germany on Rommel's behalf, laden with documents and plans. These trips are substantiated by documents listing the Lieutenant's travels that are filed in the Bundes-Militarachiv in Germany – although they make no mention of any cases that might contain valuable treasure.

In October 1942, for example, he travelled 'with letters' on a German aircraft to Mussolini's headquarters in Rome; and the following month flew to East Prussia for an audience with Hitler 'carrying secret documents' and a request from Rommel for a change in the Führer's orders. During this trip, Berndt took another flight to visit Lucie Rommel at the family home and gave her 'Rommel's suitcase of secret papers and letters'.

In total, Lieutenant Berndt had five meetings with Hitler and during at least two of these, he and the Führer were alone for a period of time. While these facts are no evidence that Berndt was carrying any gifts or stolen booty, there can be no denying he did have the opportunity to do so.

The following January, Berndt was promoted to captain. Two months later, he was recalled to Germany in the wake of the chief he had served so well. There he returned to the Propaganda Ministry to deal with the media on stories of air defence.

Alfred Berndt died in Hungary in 1945, just two months before the end of the war, apparently alone and heartbroken. The fact that he had been the man largely responsible for ensuring the fame of probably Germany's only 'hero' was completely unknown to the pair of soldiers who laid him unceremoniously in an unmarked grave.

The second man in the frame as a go–between for 'Rommel's Gold' was Corporal Albert Böttcher, the Field Marshal's secretary, who was by his side throughout the North African campaign and, like Berndt, shared his confidences. A quietly spoken, meticulous man who had been a small-town banker before the war, he was known for his discretion where Rommel and his requirements were concerned.

Unlike Berndt, however, Corporal Böttcher was only entrusted with the more mundane tasks of the Field Marshal's day-to-day life in the field, though he did keep precise shorthand notes, paying particular attention to detail. His account of the capture of Tobruk and the rewards it brought his commander is especially vivid and certainly all Rommel's biographers have reason to be grateful for the notebooks he carefully filled in each day and which are now preserved in the Militararchiv.   *Ref.*

These writing pads in his neat hand reveal that Böttcher was given the occasional out-of-the-ordinary mission by Rommel. One in particular on 13 July 1943 catches the eye immediately. The notes indicate that the Corporal flew to Germany with a number of parcels. These packages were ostensibly from Rommel for his wife's birthday – and from the evidence of her delighted letter of thanks to her husband dated the following day, contained 'the most lovely Arab bracelets, ear pendants and trinkets'.

Some of the loot from Tobruk that Rommel had captured just a month earlier, possibly? Or maybe part of a larger consignment that Böttcher was on his way to deliver to the Reich Chancellery, as the stories linking Rommel to the treasure claim? Again there is no one to answer because Albert Böttcher died in 1966.

The evidence points to there being no substance in these rumours at all. Indeed, as will become clear, it seems that the booty named after the Field Marshal has only the most tenuous connection to him. To uncover the link it is necessary to examine the story of another German officer who was also on a mission to North Africa at the same time. A battle-hardened and menacing figure named Walter Rauff.

The winter sun was high over the sparkling waters of the Mediterranean on the morning of 14 November 1942 as the dark shape of a Junkers JU86 banked over the Gulf of Tunis and made its final approach to landing at El Aouina airport.

The airfield, for some years a combined civil and military establishment used by both French and Italian commercial airlines, was now a priority base for all important German flights, especially those with missions related to the now critical North African campaign. Situated north-east of the capital, Tunis, El Aouina was connected by a five-mile stretch of road that ran straight to the outskirts of the bustling Tunisian city.

On board the flight from Berlin was SS officer *Obersturmbannführer* (Lieutenant-Colonel) Walter Rauff, a dedicated Nazi with a terrible mission. A tall, ramrod-straight man in his forties with cropped blond hair and steely blue eyes, he had been sent to the country with orders to help resolve the Jewish 'problem'.

Following the surprise landing a week earlier on 7 November of 140,000 Allied troops in the Vichy-French countries of Morocco and Algeria, the Germans had taken over control of Tunisia and were now following their own agenda. For the next six months, the country would be a battleground in every respect. As Rauff walked down the steps from the Junkers, adjusting his immaculate black uniform with its silver flashes and straightening his cap emblazoned with the unmistakable death's head badge, he gazed for the first time at the landscape that was to be his proving ground – or, if he failed, the place of his fate.

To his left he saw a stretch of glistening water which he had been told by a member of the Junkers' crew was the shallow Lac de Tunis, El Bahira ('the little sea') connected to the ocean by a narrow canal which allowed entry for shipping. The lake was also a seaplane base, but Rauff was more interested in the fact it was renowned as a good spot for fishing and shooting water fowl, both favourite pastimes of his in earlier, civilian days.

Away to the SS man's right lay the sprawl of Tunis itself, the golden roofs of the dozens of mosques glinting in the sunshine. On the flight from Berlin, Rauff had read a dossier about the place so that he was well prepared for his new domain. Then as he was driven along the dusty road towards the city in a staff car that had been sent to meet him, he silently reviewed the details in his head.

Tunis was believed to be more ancient than Carthage and for a time it had been the domain of the pirate Khair ed Din (Barbarossa). Now it was one of the country's largest ports with three well-equipped basins and dozens of piers and lifting appliances. It had been the seat of the French Resident General – as well as the headquarters for the Italian military forces – until the German takeover, Rauff had read.

According to the dossier, Tunis was the leading manufacturing centre in the country – treating minerals and manufacturing foodstuffs, olive oil, bricks, cement and textiles – and a vital link in the chain forwarding provisions and oil from ten vast storage tanks to Field Marshal Rommel's Panzer troops in neighbouring Libya. For this reason it was important for Germans always to be on the alert for sabotage or enemy bombing raids.

The population of a quarter of a million people were split almost equally between those of European extraction and those who were native born. The city itself was similarly divided into distinctive native and European sections, the former consisting of the oriental-style medina and kasba and the suburbs of Bab Souika and Bab Djazira on gently sloping foothills and the latter on reclaimed flat land on the western shore of the Lac de Tunis.

Significantly (the notes had pointed out to Rauff) a large proportion of the city's Jewish population of 27,400 people lived in the northern part of the medina and were immediately noticeable by the distinctive clothes they wore, especially the women. In the southern half of the medina, he would find the Souk el Berka, or market, which dealt in vast quantities of precious stones and jewellery. The SS man had smiled to himself when he read that the place had once been a slave market.

The European neighbourhood, sometimes called the Quartier France or Marine, was laid out in regular avenues intersected at right angles by streets running from north to south and full of hotels, banks, shops and theatres. Rauff was to be accommodated on the Avenue de Carthage where several other senior SS men were living and situated within walking distance of the Place de la Résidence and the town hall.

As his car finally pulled into the city, Rauff reflected that Tunis was at the centre of a network of good roads leading in all directions, in particular to the other main centres of population. He had no doubt that there would be much travelling to be done in the days to come.

Since the events of Walter Rauff's mission to Tunisia in the winter of 1942, there has been little research into what precisely happened. The evidence suggests, however, that his objective was to launch another phase of the infamous Nazi plan of mass extermination, the 'Final Solution', and consign the country's 60,000 Jews to the gas chambers.

The German persecution of the Jews was, in fact, already well under way by the time he arrived in Tunis, as Albert Memmi has written:

In the ghettos, the raids by German soldiers were getting more frequent. They were taking anyone: old, young, fit or sick. In desperation, the elders, aware that no help was forthcoming from anywhere – and that the Germans could easily take a whole ghetto and rumours were everywhere that Jews were to be sent to Germany – decided to strike a bargain.

If there were no more raids and medical exemption for the elderly and the sick, the Jewish people would provide a fixed contingent of workers for the work camps. In retrospect it would be easy to criticise this move, but those who did were almost all the people who had the good fortune to be able to hide outside the ghettos.

By the end of the year, the eager Rauff had visited all the major Jewish enclaves and collected a vast amount of data. But the pressure for results was mounting from his superiors in Berlin – much as it was on Rommel and his Afrika Korps.

Winston Churchill, who had always viewed the North African campaign as vital in the war against Germany, later wrote about the situation as it then was with an insider's knowledge and understanding in his masterful study, *The Second World War: The Grand Alliance* (1950):

My hopes that General Auchinleck would clear Libya in February 1943 were disappointed. He underwent a series of grievous reverses. Hitler, perhaps encouraged by this success, determined upon a large-scale fight for Tunis and presently moved above two hundred thousand fresh troops thither through Italy and across the Mediterranean. The British and American Armies therefore became involved in a larger campaign in North Africa than I had contemplated.

But the battle was not yet lost, as Churchill added:

> A delay of four months was for this reason enforced upon
> the time-table. The Anglo–American Allies did not obtain
> control of 'the whole of the North and West African
> possessions of France, and the further control by Britain of
> the whole North African shore from Tunis to Egypt' by the
> end of 1942. We obtained these results only in May 1943.

The wait was, however, worth it from Churchill's point of
view. Indeed, he believed that if Hitler had cut his losses in
North Africa he would have been able to double his forces in
France and thereby frustrate any British plans for the invasion
of Europe.

The delay did little for the plans of *Obersturmbannführer* Walter
Rauff. With news that Field Marshal Montgomery was pushing
the retreating Afrika Korps back across Libya and that they might
soon be in Tunisia, he realised he had to take action – and quickly.
Albert Memmi again fills in the details: 'The Germans became
more demanding, taking the over 35s and then the over 40s. The
communities were unable to keep up with the demand for
monthly replacement contingents and soon people were refusing
to go. The raids started again with increased brutality.'

Rauff was becoming increasingly torn between his duty and
worry for his own safety. He was aware that the American troops
who had landed in Morocco and Algeria were moving eastwards
in a giant pincer movement to meet Montgomery and the
British Eighth Army as they pushed westwards across Libya. If
they met and he fell into the hands of either, the SS man
reckoned he could expect little mercy.

It was in January 1943 that Walter Rauff made his big decision. Whether he was motivated by instructions, an attempt to wrest some success from his mission, or just plain anxiety, it is impossible to tell. The facts, though, are clear enough.

In the last week of the month, he drove 200 miles from Tunis to the strategically located town of Gabès, less than 100 miles from the Libyan border. The reason he had decided to pick on this location for what he had in mind is not difficult to determine. Rauff's dossier may well have told him that this was an area where trans-Saharan caravans had once travelled carrying gold, ivory and slaves and had been plagued by Berber highwaymen. These merciless cut-throats made a speciality of forcing any merchants they captured to drink vast quantities of hot water in order to vomit up any gold they might have swallowed.

Gabès itself had originally been the site of a Roman colony known as Tacapae and had been turned into a garrison town by the French authorities in 1936. The French had become concerned about the potential danger from Mussolini's troops in Libya attempting to expand into Tunisia. To counter this threat, they set up the Mareth Line some 23 miles to the south of the town, consisting of a 28-mile-long defence system of concrete pillboxes, wire and anti-tank ditches.

Following the German seizure of power, the Afrika Korps had set up a headquarters in the town to use as a strategic point on their supply lines to Libya. As unwilling and helpless spectators, the 18,600 inhabitants of Gabès found themselves living in a constant state of anxiety. If times under the French had been uncomfortable, life under the Germans held the threat of far worse.

The town itself consisted of two sections: one, a French-style community of low, flat-roofed houses, public buildings and a town hall, as well as a railway station with links to the north and south; the other, to the west, a separate Jewish quarter occupied by some 3,100 men, women and children. Rauff had visited the community earlier and knew that it was one of the few places in Tunisia where the Jews lived quite apart from their neighbours. Their sense of isolation and vulnerability was a factor that had become clear to him during a meeting with a group of the community leaders.

When Rauff arrived this time at the group of houses situated alongside a large oasis, he was not accompanied by his normal *Oberschführer* (Staff Sergeant) and a driver. Behind him as the staff car swept through rows of palms and small crops of olives, apricots and vines, were two trucks carrying a unit of heavily armed special commandos. As soon as he pulled up in front of the community's synagogue, Rauff summoned the senior rabbi and ordered him to convene a special meeting. The man was to ensure that all the leaders of the community – the other rabbis, businessmen and traders – attended.

There is no record of precisely what the SS man said to the assembled company of almost 100 men. It seems very probable he told them that with the battle-front drawing ever closer he was under orders to increase the numbers of Jews being taken into work camps. He may even have threatened to transport the entire Jewish population of Gabès. Whichever, the silent line of German commandos with guns slung over their shoulders standing behind him as he spoke, added to the sense of threat in his words.

What is beyond dispute is that *Obersturmbannführer* Rauff offered the men a deal. He would give them the chance to buy their freedom.

78

He knew the community was wealthy and had contacts with two other rich Jewish enclaves nearby; Sfax where there were some 3,500 Jews and Djerba with almost 5,000. Djerba was also the location of the Ghriba Synagogue, an ancient pilgrimage site and the seat of the nation's Jewish community. This, the oldest and most revered synagogue in Tunisia, was said to have been built by *Cohens* – high priests – fleeing the destruction of the First Temple in Jerusalem in 586 BC and was believed to incorporate a stone from the Temple of Solomon. Over the years, the synagogue had become fabulously wealthy with gifts of beautiful silver and gold artefacts from pilgrims and visitors.

'*Sie könnten sich mit sechzig Zentnern Gold freikaufen,*' Rauff had barked at his audience, each one silently hanging on his every word for a clue as to their fate, 'For sixty hundredweight of gold you will be free.'

The German told his listeners they had just 48 hours in which to collect the blood money. He did not mind in what form it came: gold, silver, currency, precious stones and artefacts, it was all the same. But if they failed – and he paused to indicate with a black-gloved hand the men standing behind him – they would seal the fate of every man, woman and child in the community.

How that price of freedom was collected – and from where – remains a mystery. But exactly two days after Rauff and his men had arrived in Gabès they departed from the oasis carrying six containers full of valuables, the exact worth of which has continued to be the subject of debate to this day.

It took the German convoy just over three hours to make the 86-mile journey north-west around the coast to the sprawling, grimy port of Sfax, the second town of Tunisia and

the chief port in terms of tonnage. There, with a minimum of
fuss, the containers of plunder were quickly loaded on to a
merchant ship routed to cross the Mediterranean via Sicily to
Italy, on the first stage of their journey to the Reich. Once on
the Italian mainland, the six cases were to be handed over to
a special detachment of Gestapo officers. It would be the
responsibility of these men to see the treasure safely delivered
to Berlin.

What emotions *Obersturmbannführer* Walter Rauff felt as he
watched the vessel steaming from the dockside of the Quai du
Commerce with the outline of the Iles Kerkenna and the hazy
coast of Libya away to his right can only be imagined. Later
that same day he heard that Rommel and his retreating forces
were more than halfway across Libya – and would, at their
present rate, be crossing the border back into Tunisia in less
than two months. (Ironically, the Mareth Line was to prove
the only real obstacle to Montgomery's relentless pursuit of
the Afrika Korps, forcing him into a flanking assault through
the Matmata mountains before advancing on Gabès and
capturing it in March 1943 at a cost of extensive damage to
the town.)

Whether obtaining the haul of gold earned Walter Rauff any
plaudits from his superiors after the failure of the Jewish
pogrom is not recorded. It seems unlikely, as no further trace of
him has been found. Similarly, whether the deal with the Jews
of Gabès was motivated by any kind of feelings of sympathy on
his part for their plight appears unlikely.

The one incontrovertible fact about this episode is that as the
merchant ship sailed off into the Mediterranean Sea that
January morning in 1943, neither Rauff nor anyone else

involved in the collection of the six cases of valuables now resting in the hold could have guessed they would become the centre of a worldwide legend and the hunt for a treasure known everywhere – quite erroneously, it is now clear – as 'Rommel's Gold'.

5

Treasure at the Gates of Hades

The Gulf of Sidra in Libya, almost 1,000 kilometres long and stretching in a magnificent crescent from Misratah in the west to Benghazi in the east, is one of the most beautiful stretches of coastline in all of North Africa. It is also the place where a hoard of Nazi plunder went dramatically missing while the Second World War was still raging across the country and can now be regarded as one of the earliest and most curious incidents that have created the mystery of Rommel's Gold.

Sidra consists of mile after mile of sandy beaches gently sloping from low, sandstone cliffs into the achingly blue sea. It is largely undeveloped, with Surt and As Sidr its only real centres of population, although there is also a large and rather unsightly oil terminal at Marsa al Burayqah.

Today the Gulf is perhaps best known as the homeland of the tribes of Qaddafi – whose most famous son, Colonel Muammar al-Qaddafi, became leader of Libya after ousting King Idris in a coup d'état in 1969 – and not somewhere associated with rumours of a lost treasure. Yet it was the discovery of oil in 1958 that helped transform Libya from a poor agricultural country into one of the world's leading petroleum producers, although there is still a timelessness about the place because of the endlessly shifting sands of the Sahara Desert which cover so much of the landscape.

For all its vast and inhospitable terrain – except along the coastal strip – the country is still rich in ancient history. In the past it has been occupied by Carthaginians, Romans, Arabs, Moors, Egyptians, Spaniards and, from 1911, by the Italians who held it as a colony until the Second World War. This occupation accounts for the fact that a section of the Arab population speak Italian.

Still to be seen not far from the capital, Tripoli, are the ruins of a Phoenician metropolis, Lepcis Magna, while just off the coast are traces of a huge sunken city referred to as Apollonia and believed to be of Greek or possibly even earlier origin. Recently, the discovery by an underwater diver of the figurine of a bronze ram has led to speculation that a Greek warship at least 3,000 years old lies on the floor of the Gulf of Sidra.

Not all the legends of the area are quite so enlightening. One story concerning an area just five miles north-east of Benghazi, known as the Amin Zarka or 'Blue Eye', is unnerving enough to send a chill up the spine on even the hottest day. For despite its romantic-sounding name, it is the location of underwater caves that folklore once claimed to be the site of the ancient Greek river of death, the River Styx.

According to Greek mythology, an aged man named Charon dressed in a flowing black robe ferries the shades of the dead over the Styx to the realm of Hades. He carries only the properly buried dead, and these people pay him with a coin that was placed under their tongues at the time of burial.

Some experts believe that Charon is probably the later incarnation of a much earlier god of death, the Etruscan deity,

Charun, depicted on sarcophagi as a half-human, half-animal monster, who holds aloft a hammer as he tears the dead from their families. Whatever the truth, the custom of putting a coin in the mouth of a corpse – 'Charon's obol' as it is referred to – has been practised in Greece until quite recent times.

It was near Amin Zarka – somehow appropriate considering its proximity to the fabled Stygian river – that a missing hoard of Nazi gold was first reported. The story begins in 1942 during the height of Rommel's campaign in North Africa.

The daylight hours of 26 August 1942 had been scorchingly hot at the Royal Naval Air Station at Maaten Baggush near Sollum. A desolate spot close to the Egyptian border, it stands on an escarpment rising up some 500 feet above the coastal plain to the Libyan Plateau and in a few parts is almost impossible to reach even by wheeled or tracked vehicles.

For the British servicemen based at Maaten Baggush the place was nothing like the scenes depicted on pre-war posters designed to lure tourists to this stretch of the coast. The mixture of the dark brown sand of the desert, scrub and rocks and a lack of natural covering made it a necessity to stay in the shade as much as possible; the sand was forever being lashed by the wind into any unwary eyes, mouths or nostrils. The plagues of flies and a complaint known as 'Desert Sores' only added to the daily trials and tribulations.

Throughout the previous week, the station had been regularly subjected to attacks by the *Khamseen*, one of the notorious hot, very dry and sand-laden winds that blow from the Sahara and can raise the temperature in a matter of hours to around 50°C. As usual it had brought clouds of sand, restricting mobility and clogging the mechanism of any vehicles and weapons that had not been completely covered. The previous day – though the fact brought scant relief to the men at Maaten Baggush – the thermometers on the station had registered a high of only 46°C.

Mercifully, as darkness fell, the *Khamseen* had subsided and the mercury had fallen to a manageable level by the time a clock ticked midnight and a group of yawning airmen were summoned from their tents to the station's briefing room. En route they passed the trio of Mark I Swordfish aircraft, all carefully swathed with tarpaulins, that they had been flying during the past six months in missions against German and Italian shipping heading for the enemy-occupied ports of Benghazi and Tobruk.

Although there were some who believed that the Fairey Swordfish torpedo bomber – first flown in 1934 – was already outdated by the time the war began, the men who had been operating in the aircraft for the past three years felt quite differently. The three-seat biplane with its iron frame and fabric covering had not only proved itself a highly effective strike weapon, but was to remain in front-line service throughout the entire conflict.

The Swordfish may have been known universally by its crews as the 'Stringbag' because of the criss-cross maze of wires between its upper and lower wings, but this was always said by the men with a mixture of affection and admiration. Thirteen squadrons of the aircraft were already in service at the start of the war – thirteen more would follow before its end – and the Swordfish had not only been the first aircraft to carry out an airborne torpedo attack, but also the first plane in the Fleet Air Arm to sink a U-boat.

Powered by a single 690hp Bristol Pegasus engine, the Mark I could carry a crew of three – a pilot, observer and radio operator/gunner – and had a top speed of 138mph with a range of 546 miles. The Swordfish carried a deadly punch with its two .303 Vickers machine guns – one firing forwards and the other rear-mounted for handling by the gunner – as well as its capability to fire eight 27kg (60lb) rockets. It could also be armed with one 730kg (1,610lb) torpedo, one 680kg (1,500lb) mine or an equivalent load of bombs.

The Swordfish had already earned its spurs in the Mediterranean before the mission from Maaten Baggush on 27 August. In November 1940, a group of the torpedo bombers based in North Africa had decimated the Italian fleet at Taranto and followed this with a number of successful raids from Malta on Axis shipping.

Only a few weeks before this latest mission, the story was being repeated all over the station of one 'Stringbag' which had been so badly damaged by enemy anti-aircraft fire in a mission over Libya that it had returned to base minus virtually all of its lower wing. Yet – so the account had it – such was the plane's capability to fly, that it had been successfully flown all the way back from the Western Desert to Britain for repairs!

When the nine aircrew sat down in the station office a few minutes after midnight, they once again found themselves listening to a success story for the Swordfish. The speaker was not the station commander nor one of his assistant officers as they had expected, but a tall, neatly dressed man who was introduced to them as Staff Captain Michael Thomas from Naval Intelligence in Cairo.

Just a week earlier, on 22 August, the captain began without any attempt at a preamble, three Mark Is operating from just up the coast had attacked some Italian warships at anchor in the port of Bomba Bay in Libya. As a result, a destroyer, two submarines and a submarine tender had been sunk. With just three torpedoes (the man added without a hint of smugness) four vessels had gone down, the destroyer having been hit when the tender exploded.

The success of this mission had made Naval Intelligence decide in conjunction with the Navy and RAF chiefs to step up aerial operations against all enemy shipping passing along the Libyan coast. The next target was to be a convoy of Axis ships that was reported to be heading for the port of Tobruk.

As the captain paused and turned to a map of North Africa pinned on the wall behind him, the nine men looked from one to another. Somehow they sensed this was going to be no ordinary mission.

Jabbing a finger at the coast of Cyrenaica, Captain Thomas said that the weather forecasters had been keeping a close eye on conditions in the area during the past 48 hours and had decided that tonight offered probably the best – possibly even the last – chance of success before the ships reached Tobruk.

As the crew members had been crossing the desert airstrip to the briefing, none of them could have failed to notice the clear, bright night sky with a haloed moon hanging over Egypt – ideal conditions for flying over the Gulf of Sidra and perfect for spotting an enemy convoy.

Earlier in the evening, Captain Thomas went on, the RAF had dispatched a wing of Wellington bombers to try to sink the merchantmen and the two destroyers protecting them. One of the ships in the convoy, the *Serina*, which particularly interested the NID, had slipped away from the others during the attack and was now believed to be on a quite different course, heading for Benghazi, some two hundred miles to the west. It was a modern vessel of 5,365 tons and believed to have an experienced Merchant Navy skipper at the helm.

The Wellingtons, of course, had neither the range nor the fuel to pursue the ship, he added, and as it was imperative to put the *Serina* to the bottom of the sea, the task was being handed to the trio of Swordfish.

However, just before any of the puzzled crew members could ask *why* the ship was so special, the captain held up his hand. No, he could not divulge why it was so necessary to sink the vessel, or even what its cargo might be. Captain Thomas looked at each of the nine men in turn before speaking again.

'Gentlemen,' he said, 'it is vital that you sink the *Serina*. She must be sent to the bottom of the ocean as far out to sea as possible before she reaches Benghazi. Get in as close as you can – she is not carrying oil or anything explosive. Just make sure there is no chance of her being salvaged.'

As the man from Naval Intelligence sat down without another word, his place was taken by the station commander who briefed the three groups of airmen. They were to take off at 1 a.m. and fly to the oasis station at Bab-es-Serir, a journey of about two hours. There they would refuel before making the onward flight to Benghazi and their target.

The commander offered a strong word of warning to the men. They should avoid the area of Amin Zarka as Rommel's headquarters were nearby. They would recognise the place from a tall radio mast the Afrika Korps engineers had erected – not to mention the murderous flak that would rise up to greet them if they were spotted.

With the merest suggestion of a grin on his face, the officer – who had apparently been a classics master at an English public school before the war – offered the nine another piece of information drawn from his knowledge of ancient history. They would, he said, be flying and fighting over the mouth of Greek mythology's river of death, the Styx.

In the next half hour, the airfield at Maaten Baggush became a scene of frantic activity after the torpor of the day.

The nine crewmen barely had time to speculate about the secrecy of their mission as they kitted up and watched the three Swordfish aircraft rolled out by gangs of mechanics to the hard standing at the end of the runway. As the planes were being given final checks, another team of ground staff drove a truck along the airstrip lighting flares for the take-off. The small lights winked against the dunes and escarpments of the desert landscape, mirroring the countless stars in the heavens above.

Precisely at one o'clock, the Pegasus engines burst into life and the three biplanes with their grey camouflage and unmistakable RAF roundels powered one after another down the runway and rose into the sky, heading west. Below each hung the unmistakable outline of a red-tipped 1,610lb torpedo almost half the planes' length.

The three Swordfish flew steadily side by side, each maintaining a speed of 125mph at just under 2,000 feet. Below lay the vastness of the Libyan desert; the three observers had to keep their eyes firmly on their compasses to make sure they did not miss the tiny, palm-shrouded oasis of Bab-es-Serir.

Refuelling of the aircraft was performed as efficiently as possible by the ground staff who had to filter the petrol out of the storage barrels to avoid getting sand into the engines of the aircraft. None of the crew members left their seats as the job was completed.

Before the trio took off again just before 3.30 a.m., each was given a weather report over the radio. A depression was apparently moving in towards the coast of Libya from the central Mediterranean and clouds and high winds were expected around daylight. None of the pilots fancied being in the air too long if another *Khamseen* were to blow up.

Radio silence was maintained between the three 'Stringbags' as they neared the coast, dropping ever closer to ground level to avoid being spotted. After taking a wide detour of the 'Blue Eye', the planes headed out for the sea lanes to the north of Benghazi.

The first sighing wind of an approaching storm had arisen and the cloud base was dropping rapidly when one of the Swordfish pilots spotted the hulk of a lone ship moving towards the Libyan coast. It was just after 5 a.m. and dawn would soon be breaking on the horizon.

As the three British torpedo bombers drew nearer, their crews had no doubt this was the *Serina* and she was about ten miles from Benghazi, moving quickly. The trio had arrived just in time.

Together the planes manoeuvred themselves into an ideal attacking position in the lowering clouds. They wanted the ship to be silhouetted against the waning moon so that it made the clearest possible target.

Despite the fact that this was a tried and tested procedure for attacks at sea, on this particular morning it went terribly wrong. Just as the Swordfish were about to dive on their prey, the cloud cover broke and all three pilots found themselves in clear sight of the *Serina*.

Before any of the aircraft had a chance to react, a flurry of ack-ack fire began to break around them. It was immediately clear from the sheer weight and ferocity of the fire that the vessel was not armed with the usual Bofors guns of a merchantman. The ship was obviously heavily defended – but what could she be carrying to require such armament?

There was no time for guessing as the three pilots took immediate avoiding action. If the Swordfish had one fault, it was its low top speed. Even calling on the maximum 138mph was not enough to prevent some of the enemy shells striking two of the aircraft.

The plane that had been designated to launch the attack turned sharply in toward the vessel, zigzagging from side to side in an effort to avoid the flak, and headed straight for the target. Courageously, the pilot held his course to get the best possible aim for his torpedo. But he held it just a moment too long. A direct hit on his fuel tank sent the plane plummeting into the sea, an exploding ball of flame.

In the meantime, the two other aircraft had taken advantage of their colleague's selfless sacrifice to close in on the *Serina* from opposite sides. Both men were now in no doubt that the captain and crew must be very anxious to get this vessel and its cargo – whatever it might be – safely to Benghazi.

Veering in from either side of the ship, the two remaining 'Stringbags' took up the attack. One, its forward guns blazing, screamed in on the port side, but again ran into a savage barrage of fire. The plane careered on wildly over the ship, the pilot obviously dead at the stick, until it, too, fell in a sheet of flame into the waters of the Gulf of Sidra.

The third plane, however, reaped the benefit from the diversions caused by the other two. Closing from the opposite bow, the pilot was able to fly his machine straight towards the *Serina* and release his torpedo with the pinpoint accuracy that hundreds of hours of flying a Swordfish had given him. Then, wrenching hard on the stick, the man pulled his throttle full out and made a screaming, shuddering, stomach-churning 180-degree turn towards what remained of the cloud cover.

The surviving Swordfish had barely climbed out of ack-ack range before a massive explosion lit up the grey morning sky. It was a sight that its three crew members were familiar with – but were perhaps more relieved to see than on any previous occasion. They had hit the target.

Reaching a height of 1,500 feet, the plane turned so that the men could all get a view of the drama being played out below them. The vessel had been struck amidships and flames were beginning to lick out of the hold. As the silent trio watched, they could see that it had been crippled beyond repair and was virtually stationary in the water.

Easing back on the throttle, the pilot of the Swordfish circled his stricken victim. He wanted to be quite sure of the *Serina*'s fate before sending a radio message back to Maaten Baggush. The passing moments turned into minutes and the only sound to be heard in the aircraft was the comforting throb of the Pegasus engine.

Then, finally, it was possible to see lifeboats being feverishly lowered from the deck of the holed ship. Her bow was beginning to lift and there could be no doubt she was going down. As the pilot watched this final act of the drama he shouted to his radio operator in the cockpit behind: 'Send a message. The target has been torpedoed and she's on fire and sinking.'

He paused and then added in a voice filled with a mixture of anger and remorse, 'You'd better tell them the other two have had it.'

Unfortunately, few details remain about the six men who gave their lives on the mission to sink the *Serina* or the three who survived after limping in their battered Swordfish back to the mainland. There are lists of Royal Navy airmen who flew the 'Stringbags' in the North African campaign and died on active service, but none whose activities I have been able to discover match the facts of this incident.

Indeed, details about the whole episode are scanty and much of the information we have comes from a report filed on 28 August 1942 by Staff Captain Michael Thomas to the NID in Cairo. Later, it was transmitted to headquarters in London and may well have crossed Ian Fleming's desk. The memo does, though, help to solve the mystery of the German merchantman's cargo that the Allies were so keen to see sent to the bottom of the Gulf of Sidra.

The events in North Africa following Rommel's lightning conquest of Libya and his progress to the border of Egypt before being thwarted by Montgomery quickly put the sinking of the *Serina* to the back of almost everyone's minds. But not quite all, for there were a handful of people – all Germans and members of the Afrika Korps – who apparently knew rather more about the sunken ship and its cargo and wanted to claim it once the war was over.

Although the bulk of the merchantman's contents were, it seems, a large consignment of provisions for the troops at the front, ranging from clothing to tinned food and cigarettes, there were also six carefully sealed steel boxes. They were said to contain gold, various paper currencies and other items worth *in excess of six million pounds sterling.*

The stories about what happened to these boxes after the sinking of the *Serina* differ considerably and all are very debatable. The version most generally told is that they must have gone to the bottom of the sea with the ship, which was lost approximately five to six miles off the coast of Benghazi, according to reports of the incident.

In a variation of the same story, the location is given as just off Tripoli. However, this is considered unlikely and is in all probability a piece of subterfuge by those who might just have more precise details of the sinking and be anxious to divert others away from the actual spot.

A second story suggests that some, if not all, of the cases were taken off the sinking merchantman by a group of crew members who escaped in a lifeboat. The sheer weight of these boxes and the difficulty of lowering them from the deck of a floundering and burning vessel puts a question mark over just how many could have been successfully moved.

The third story claims that the steel boxes were saved and taken on a motorised boat that was fortuitously on board the *Serina* into the Gulf of Sidra. Here they were buried in one of the numerous shallow *wadis* that can be found along the deserted coast. The motorboat was then scuttled and the fortune left for reclamation later.

Nothing more was heard of the six cases until 1946. Then, according to an American journalist, Kurt Singer, who investigated the rumours for *True: The Man's Magazine*, the whole business surfaced again. In an article entitled 'The Lost Nazi Gold of Libya', complete with a photograph of a group of men standing beside an ex-RAF Land Rover in the Libyan desert, he wrote: 'These men have dedicated their lives to searching for the missing gold. They are all ex-soldiers of the Afrika Korps who were taken prisoners of war by the British and worked for the RAF as maintenance men. They believe the bullion is buried somewhere along the coast of Libya.'

Singer had his own explanation of the origin of the gold, however. He claimed that after the battle of El Alamein the Germans had collected together all the gold in the Italian-Libyan banks in Tobruk and decided to ship it away to prevent it falling into British hands. But because of the growing Allied strength in the air and at sea, the booty had never reached its destination. It had last been seen, Singer wrote, in armoured cars disappearing into the desert, which the ex-POWs were now trying to trace.

Not surprisingly, this motley crew were no more lucky in their search than Singer in trying to trace the real history of the missing gold. In fact, they were looking in the wrong place and he had got hold of the wrong end of the story.

It is worth mentioning at this stage before putting the record straight, that six metal boxes have subsequently been seen in the waters of the Gulf of Sidra. They were spotted in 1962 by an experienced English scuba diver, Robin Leigh, while he was serving in the British Army at RAF Tobruk. His job was the protection of the air base and harbour installations from terrorist attacks.

However, as he recalled later, life there in the early sixties was pretty peaceful. Feelings of goodwill between the British and the Libyans were strong and the dangers of attack minimal, giving men like Leigh plenty of time to pursue their own interests.

One weekend, he and a group of friends took a trip on a long-range truck along the coast westward towards Benghazi. In one small coastal *wadi* which they stopped to explore, Leigh made a most remarkable discovery. Describing his experiences in *Diver* magazine in May 2002, he wrote:

In two years I had seen many things beneath the Libyan waters – Roman wine jars, an Italian field gun and several aircraft, including a Junkers 87 so deep that even with a scuba it was out of reach, yet visible from the surface. But that day I saw something that still puzzles me today.

Near the headland, the water shelved away quickly to turn blue-black with distance. That was when I found myself looking at some large square objects set in an apparently logical pattern. When I went down I found myself at 24m standing on top of a steel box with sloping sides. Next to it was another, and then several more set in pairs to form an underwater avenue leading out to sea.

Because of the depth, Leigh – who had left his aqualung behind and was snorkelling – soon found himself short of breath and had to return to the surface. Four more times he went down to look at the mysterious objects and each time returned to the surface gasping for air and even more puzzled.

After the last of these dives, Leigh went to find two of his fellow squaddies who were swimming near a cliff ledge and told them what he had found. When he suggested all three take a look, one of the men pointed out that the sun was already sinking and because the area was known still to be mined from the war, it was important for them to get back on the Benghazi road before dark. They could always come back another weekend with aqualungs, the man said – but another opportunity never arose for Leigh before he was transferred to Aden.

In the months that followed, Robin Leigh continued to wonder what the boxes might be. Turrets removed from armoured cars, perhaps? Mooring blocks for ships, possibly? Even ammunition boxes fallen from a ship? All of these ideas seemed unlikely to him.

However, a chance sighting of the *True* magazine story about the ex-Afrika Korps men searching for the six missing cases of gold in the same vicinity brought him up short. Could *this* be the answer to his mystery?

'What fired me up was the photo of two of the Germans in the group,' he wrote. 'I knew them! Several times they had stumbled across our remote weekend camps, claiming that they were just searching the old battlefields for ammunition for their Luger pistols. I had even given them a box of British Army 9mm bullets so that they could pop away at snakes.'

The course of Robin Leigh's own life – and Libya's changing attitude towards Britain since Colonel Qaddafi's rise to power – has prevented him from returning to try and find the spot again. At the time of writing, though, he still nurses the hope of one day accompanying an expedition to look for those steel boxes.

Which brings me to the revelation about the real nature of the Libyan treasure trove. Although it, too, has been linked to the name of Rommel, it is a quite different hoard intended for a different purpose to the loot spirited out of Tunisia and bound for Berlin. The fate of *that* treasure in fact lies hundreds of miles away off the coastline of a small island, as we shall discover.

The secret of the six steel boxes on the *Serina* that the Germans were so desperate to get to North Africa – and the British equally desperate to stop – was that they contained funds destined *for* Rommel, rather than the other way around.

The confirmation of this fact is to be found in Captain Michael Thomas's report to Naval Intelligence. Thanks to spies working for the Allies, his department had learned about the *Serina*'s imminent arrival in Libya with wealth from Germany to finance Rommel's campaign in North Africa.

The £6 million was to pay the Field Marshal's troops and, once he was in Cairo, to buy Intelligence and support for the Nazi cause throughout the Middle East. It is believed that much of the money had been looted from banks and safe deposit boxes belonging to wealthy men and women – many of them probably Jews – in countries conquered by the Germans, and diverted for use in the war effort.

Further details about this operation came to light in documents seized later by the British Army during the invasion of Italy. The discovery was made in Rome at the headquarters of the Italian Naval Intelligence Department. Here a vast collection of papers provided detailed information about the workings of the German and Italian war machines during their ill-fated union.

One small file among all these papers contained details of the *Serina*, her skipper, a Captain Carlo Tacchini, her route to North Africa and her precious cargo. Also, typed in underlined capitals, the simple facts of her fate.

That these papers should have survived is remarkable in itself. For when the Allies were nearing Rome, it is not unreasonable to assume that orders would have been given for their destruction because of their sensitive nature.

They avoided this fate because of an even more extraordinary series of events and, in particular, the skill of a notorious Scottish safe-cracker who was then in the employ of the British Army. His name was John Ramensky and his exploits provide the next step in our attempt to solve the whereabouts of the 'real' Rommel's Gold.

6

The Prince of Safe-crackers

Johnny Ramensky was a tough, streetwise career criminal from Glasgow who, as a result of his extraordinary activities, became known throughout Scotland as 'The Prince of Safe-crackers'. He was also the first in a series of larger-than-life characters to become involved in the hunt for Rommel's Gold.

At first glance, Ramensky might seem an unlikely person to feature in the mystery of the Nazi gold. But in fact his particular skills made him ideally suited for a special search-and-find mission on which he was dispatched with a group of British Commandos in 1943 during the Allied conquest of Italy.

As the British and American troops rolled across the country putting Mussolini's troops and their German allies to flight, Allied Intelligence chiefs were anxious to seize as many Axis documents and plans as possible before they were destroyed. And they were not just interested in battle plans, but also any papers that referred to art treasures and valuables – especially gold and silver bullion – that had been plundered by the enemy. These documents were believed to be hidden in sealed rooms and large safes, often hastily abandoned by their former owners. If they could be found intact, they would need to be opened without destroying or damaging the contents – which is where Johnny Ramensky came in.

From the evidence of wartime Scottish police records it seems clear that officers on the force regarded Ramensky with a mixture of anger at his recurring villainy and also a certain affection. For despite his notoriety and lengthy criminal record, Johnny was a likeable character with a spirit and vitality that marked him out as being rather different from the other hardmen of the Scottish underworld in the violent 1920s and 1930s.

In fact, Ramensky was not by birth a Scot at all. He had been born in Lithuania in 1902, the son of a coal miner who had emigrated to Scotland four years afterwards in the hope of finding a better life for himself and his family. Tragically, this hope was dashed when the man died and his desperate widow was forced to move into the notorious Gorbals slums. Here she managed to scratch a living working in a weaving mill.

Mrs Ramensky's son, whose original Christian name proved unpronounceable to the other slum kids, was soon known to everyone as 'Johnny'. Like many children in Glasgow at the time, he became a member of a local street mob, joining the Black Hand Gang. These 'Neds' – as the violent and anti-social gangs whose members ranged from pre-teens to men in their early thirties were known – lived by thieving and used violence to control their streets: fists, bottles and knives were their favourite weapons. There were many bloody pitched battles between the Black Hand Gang and their great rivals, the Redskins, and by the age of ten Johnny Ramensky had learned to look after himself on the city's streets.

By his own account, Johnny had his first run-in with the local 'busies' – as the police were known – when he was ten. He was arrested while riding a stolen bicycle, a means of transport that was a rare sight in the heart of the Gorbals. The youngster was not at all intimidated by the towering policeman. 'A friend lent it tae me,' he said using the quick thinking that would get him out of many tight corners in the future, 'I didnae ken it was stolen.'

Johnny refused to squeal on his friend and put on one of his cheekiest smiles. The constable, obviously amused by the young guttersnipe, let him off with a warning.

The man's good advice fell on deaf ears, however. Soon Ramensky was following the lead of older members of the Black Hand Gang, taking part in petty thieving and receiving the usual 'old lag' apprenticeship of reformatory school, Borstal and prison. After one spell in Borstal, Johnny decided to take notice of his mother's appeals to get a job. His size and fitness made mining an obvious choice and for a couple of years he worked in a Lanarkshire coalfield. His intelligence and willingness to learn gained him the chance of a more responsible job: firing explosive charges as new coal seams were opened up deep in the mine. Ramensky's job description was 'shot-firer' – and the skill he developed was to lead not to a successful mining career but to serving more than forty of his sixty years in prison.

The allure of crime with which Johnny had grown up was too strong for him and in 1921 he was caught house-breaking and sentenced to five years. He put the time behind bars to good use, however, devoting himself to keeping fit. He spent hours developing his muscles in the exercise yard and was admired by prisoners and guards alike for his ability to walk on his hands for fifteen minutes at a stretch – including a climb up 30 steps to his cell.

After eighteen months, Johnny Ramensky was released for good behaviour and married his childhood sweetheart, Mary McManus. However, when he took to returning home regularly with a piece of jewellery or an item of furniture for his new bride, the reason for all his exercising became obvious – it had been to keep himself fit for cat-burgling activities. When Johnny was tracked home by the police after one night of such activities his Gorbals flat was found to be almost completely furnished with 'gifts'. This time he was given three months hard labour.

In the years between 1925 and 1934 Ramensky earned a reputation as one of the cleverest cat burglars in Scotland. He was nevertheless caught three times, and received sentences totalling six years – but his notoriety also earned him regular stories in the Scottish press. In one front-page feature in the *Glasgow Herald*, 'a friend' was quoted as saying: 'There was no roof or wall which could defeat Johnny.'

And that, in a nutshell, became Johnny Ramensky's problem. Whenever a seemingly impossible burglary was committed, the first person the police thought of as a suspect was the cat burglar from the Gorbals.

It was after his release from prison in 1933 that Ramensky decided to change his *modus operandi*. House-breaking paid peanuts compared with safe-breaking and he had learned to be an expert with explosives while working as a shot-firer. Within a matter of months he had become a skilled opportunist and blown several factory safes, getting away with thousands of pounds.

Percy Sillitoe, the gang-busting policeman from Sheffield who had been appointed Chief Constable of Glasgow in 1931, soon became aware of the activities of Johnny Ramensky. Yet, in time, Sillitoe came to hold a sneaking regard for the safe-cracker's versatility and skill – and would later be influential in turning this talent to the good of the country. Sillitoe understood the secret of Ramensky's special skill with gelignite, the extremely effective explosive containing nitroglycerine, guncotton, powdered wood and sodium nitrate, and wrote later in his autobiography, *Cloak Without Dagger*: 'His basic formula was to use the smallest amount of explosives possible. He had a genius for knowing the exact fraction he needed to make the least possible noise and only wreck the section of the safe he wanted to wreck.'

Once again, though, Ramensky as good as left his fingerprints on a brilliant safe-cracking job at Clydebank where he got away with over £5,000. Sillitoe's detectives followed the trail to Johnny's door, arrested him, and gave compelling evidence which earned him a five-year penal sentence at tough Peterhead Prison in Aberdeen.

The jail, built in 1888, had the reputation of being the Alcatraz of Scotland. The fourteen-foot walls were so steep as to be unscalable, while the building itself was partly moated by the River Don. It was claimed that no one had ever escaped. Johnny was about to change all that.

Ramensky continued with his arduous keep–fit regime. Then one morning he was informed that his wife, Mary, was dangerously ill and asked permission to visit her. The governor turned the request down flat. Consumed with anger, Johnny determined to do what no other prisoner had done before and began making plans to escape. Choosing a bitterly cold night and wearing only his underpants he first climbed a thin gas pipe. It then took him half an hour to work his way across the iron rafters of the prison roof before forcing a skylight window and swinging himself over the outside wall.

Ramensky then climbed up the girders below the bridge across the River Don to the mainland and painstakingly hauled himself from one to the next until he reached the other side. Every shivering, agonising inch of the crossing had been made possible by the hours of exercise he had undertaken in the prison.

For the next two days Johnny remained hidden in a garage, waiting for an opportunity to get some food and clothes. Unfortunately he was spotted and was soon arrested and on his way back to Peterhead. On his arrival, he was thrown into solitary confinement and his legs put in shackles, so furious were the authorities that their reputation for invincibility had been shattered.

The stories of Ramensky's escape and survival in his underwear were soon common knowledge across Scotland. His toughness and audacity even came to the attention of MPs in the House of Commons in London who were outraged at the use of shackles on a prisoner. A bill was subsequently passed forbidding their use in Scotland.

Despite his incredible show of bravado, there was to be no happy ending for Johnny Ramensky. His wife died shortly before his release from solitary confinement and he remained bitter about the circumstances for years afterwards. However, neither Mary's death nor the time added to his sentence did anything to change Ramensky's attitude towards crime when he came out of Peterhead in 1938. In the next few months, a number of safes were robbed in places as far apart as Edinburgh and Manchester, all blown with the silent efficiency of a master.

One of the most daring of these break-ins occurred at a laundry in Aberdeen just before the premises were due to open on a July morning. Two safes were broken into and approximately £300 stolen. One of the safes had been forced open by explosives, it transpired, while the other had been opened with a key found inside the first. The money had been taken from envelopes left strewn all over the floor amid a scattering of sawdust and alum used in packing the exploded safe.

Almost as soon as the police had guessed that the raid was probably the handiwork of the Prince of Safe-crackers, they received information that a man answering his description had hired a taxi at a stand not far from the laundry. Further clues pointed to this same man having travelled via Perth to Glasgow. Photographs of several criminals, including that of Johnny Ramensky, were shown to witnesses and none had any hesitation in identifying him.

The following day Ramensky was arrested and charged with the laundry raid. Forensic evidence comparing the mixture of substances found at the crime scene with tiny samples in the safe-cracker's trouser turn-ups and between the soles and uppers of his shoes left Lord Russell, the judge at his trial, in no doubt as to his guilt. But like so many others before him, Russell found himself curiously affected by Ramensky's contradictory nature. In passing a sentence of five years' imprisonment, he concluded: 'I am sure that a man of your ability could earn a livelihood in some honest way.' The judge had no idea just how true these words were to prove.

The world that Johnny Ramensky found when he quite legitimately crossed the Peterhead Prison bridge in bright sunlight on a cold October morning in 1943 was utterly different from the one he had left five years earlier. A war was now on and the very existence of Britain was threatened by the all-conquering Nazi forces ranged around the nation's shores on the Atlantic Ocean and just across the English Channel in France.

Ramensky had, of course, been following the progress of the war in prison in the newspapers and on the radio, but such events had seemed very distant to a man still absorbed in obsessive exercise. He was to discover a great deal more about the reality of it as soon as he was over the bridge.

A police car with two officers was parked at the roadside. If his heart skipped a beat, Johnny did not let it show. The driver raised a finger in his direction. 'Hey, Johnny,' the man said with the familiarity of someone who had met Ramensky many times before. 'Inspector Westland wants a wee word with ye.'

The two policemen and their passenger sat in silence as the car was driven to Aberdeen police station, Ramensky deep in his own thoughts. He had done his time. What on earth did they want him for *now*?

The mystery was not long in being resolved once the ex-jailbird and the inspector sat facing each other across a desk. The British Army needed men with Johnny's special skill in handling explosives, Westland told him, and at the moment were not too particular where they came from.

Evidence now available suggests that it was Percy Sillitoe who had earmarked Ramensky for this work. The Chief Constable may, of course, have seen it as one way of getting a persistent criminal off the streets, but he was certainly influential in seeing Johnny recruited into the British Special Forces, the Commandos as they were more commonly known. Whatever the case, Johnny soon found himself cracking safes for the national good rather than against it. According to Sillitoe's biographer, A W Cockerill, in *Sir Percy Sillitoe* (1975):

> During the Second World War, he [Ramensky] made a number of parachute drops into occupied territory on secret service missions. According to James McGlinchey who first met Sillitoe in 1939 and wrote a series of reports on his activities, it was Sillitoe who recommended Ramensky for this work. Richard Sillitoe recalls his father mentioning Ramensky's war work long after the family left Glasgow and there was no reason why Percy Sillitoe should have known anything about the safe-cracker's war activities unless he himself had been involved in some way.

It seems likely that with his record, Johnny felt he had no option but to accept the proposal. He was under no illusions that once at liberty he would probably return to crime and if he turned down Westland's offer, the police would undoubtedly throw the book at him the next time he was caught. So he accepted – and events moved quickly thereafter.

Ramensky was first introduced to Brigadier Robert 'Lucky' Laycock, the chief of British Special Forces, who explained how they wanted to make use of his special talents in undercover operations in Occupied Europe. Laycock also delivered a no-nonsense lecture about his patriotic duty and warned him that the Army could be even tougher than the police with those who broke the rules.

Johnny's initial training took place at the Commandos' tough training centre at Achnacarry on Loch Arkaig in the Highlands.

Later he was transferred to Dorset where he was given an intensive course in explosives. Within days, however, Ramensky was virtually playing the teacher himself, giving the other new Commandos tips on how to explode safes without wrecking their contents. There was no need for him to explain to anyone just how he knew so much – the twinkle in his eye as he skilfully packed gelignite into the keyholes of one old safe after another and blew it open, was a clear enough indication of a lifetime of unlawful activities.

Just over six months later, in June 1944, Ramensky was sent on his first mission when he was parachuted into Italy behind the German lines. As he fell to earth in the mountains near Pontecorvo, he was picked up by a group of Italian partisans and half a dozen Commandos led by Major James Hawkins who had arrived earlier. The officer wasted no time in briefing him.

Hawkins explained that their target was the German Embassy in Rome. The group was to go in ahead of the Allied forces who were advancing from the south and try to grab vital documents before they were taken away or destroyed by the embassy staff. It had come to the attention of British Intelligence that all operational saboteurs in Italy were being supplied from the embassy and a list of their names would be the least of the secrets they hoped to find in the building. Ramensky was handed a map of the embassy which he saw contained four strongrooms and twelve safes. His task was to open them all.

Ten days later, under the cover of a starless night, the Commandos slipped into Rome and silently entered the embassy compound. Ramensky effortlessly opened a big iron padlock into the main building and stepped inside.

Unerringly, Johnny moved down a flight of steps into a darkened cellar. Snapping on his torch, he let out a low whistle of surprise. The room was packed to the ceiling with high explosives. On the floor were rows of metal drums filled with TNT, plastic explosives and gelignite, while around the walls in neat rows lay all kinds of fuses, switches, incendiary gadgets and booby-trap devices. No one could be in any doubt as to the purpose of this deadly cache.

Now that Major Hawkins had confirmed his suspicions, he ordered Ramensky to go upstairs into the strongrooms and open all the safes. Johnny decided to use his favoured small powder charges, and within half an hour had opened all twelve. Inside were stacked a priceless hoard of documents about the Germans' sabotage plans, along with the names of their agents throughout Italy. Most important of all was a folder of papers – many of them encrypted orders from Berlin – dealing with plans for the German withdrawal from Italy.

Having completed their mission, Ramensky and the rest of the Commandos and partisans withdrew as silently as they had come back into the hills where they remained to await the arrival of the Allied armies. Once Rome had been taken, Johnny was kept busy for several weeks opening all the other safes used by the Germans. For the first time in his life he could happily indulge his greatest passion without the fear of the arm of the law tapping him on the shoulder at any moment.

As the Allies moved northwards from Rome, Major Hawkins and his men were assigned to further missions behind enemy lines. Several had to be aborted, however, because of poor weather or the capture of partisans who were to be their guides. On one occasion, Ramensky recalled flying over an area where they were due to be dropped when a sharp-eyed Commando realised the flares which had been lit were different from normal and that the Germans were clearly waiting to give them an unwelcome reception.

Following several more false starts, the group were moved to the coastal town of Livorno where it was decided to travel on foot to their next destination, La Spezia, a major port on the Ligurian Sea, close to the northern border of Tuscany. Huge German guns were known to be hidden in the nearby Alpi Apaun mountains blocking the Allied advance and it was vital to obtain information about their strength and location. Major Hawkins decided to send a small advance party of ten men – seven Commandos led by Lieutenant Wilfred Crandall plus three partisans who knew the area well.

The facts about La Spezia spoke volumes as to its importance. Protected on three sides by steeply rising terrain that shielded it from the most hazardous weather conditions, the port had developed rapidly after the building of a naval dockyard with inner and outer harbours was completed in 1865. It was now said to be the largest naval base in Italy.

Thanks to its position in a natural inlet at the head of the Golfo di La Spezia, the anchorages and berths in the port were so sheltered that ships never had to be moved when strong northerly winds or high waves struck and sailing inside the breakwater had never been cancelled by bad conditions. The base could accommodate over forty medium- to deep-draft vessels and had special facilities in an inner harbour for submarines.

La Spezia had already been the target of Allied night-time bombing – which would ultimately cause terrible damage and necessitate extensive rebuilding after the war – but was still in regular use by the Germans. The reputation of the occupiers, however, had been blackened in the eyes of many local people because of their ruthless looting of works of art and other valuables throughout the area.

The objective of the group led by Lieutenant Crandall was to penetrate into La Spezia and find the German command post. According to Major Hawkins – who planned to reinforce Crandall's group as soon as they were in situ – there was another large and important safe in the Nazi HQ. The partisans had told him that because the Germans believed their position to be impregnable, the safe was packed with highly sensitive information about many of the enemy's activities in Italy and North Africa. Even without any idea what this material might be, John Ramensky rubbed his hands with anticipation at the chance of some more juicy safe-cracking.

Each of Lieutenant Crandall's men was issued with special equipment for their mission to La Spezia: a map of the area printed on silk, a pistol with silencer and ample ammunition, plus an escape kit containing a saw, a tiny compass and a fistful of Italian lire. Ramensky contented himself with his faithful explosives kit.

The three partisans led the group safely through the mountainous country along the west coast of Italy, taking care to keep clear of the retreating German troops. They passed the towns of Viareggio, Massa and Carrara until finally they were in sight of La Spezia. It was a long and gruelling trip, even for a fit man like Ramensky, and when the group's supplies of food ran low they had to feed themselves on the occasional stray goat or chicken killed with the silenced guns. The tough little Scotsman never forgot the devastation he saw in the countryside. In

Rommel – 'The Desert Fox' – after whom one of the most
famous lost treasures of the Second World War is named.

Right: Hitler dreamed of creating the greatest museum of treasures in the world as his memorial.

Below: Sketch by Roderick Frick for the Führermuseum in Linz.

A selection of the valuables looted by the Nazis for Hitler's Führermuseum.

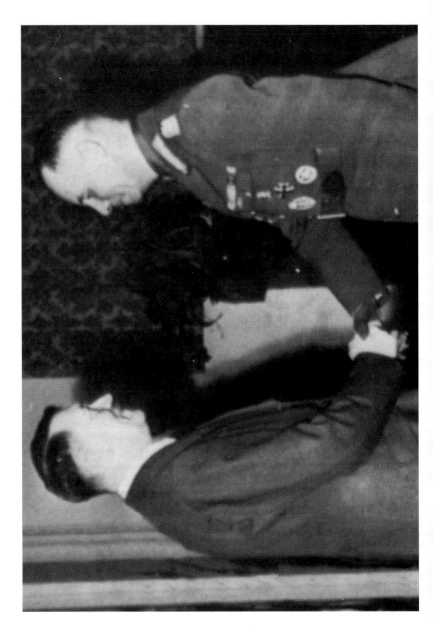

Right: The story of Rommel's Gold was featured by Ian Fleming in his James Bond adventure, *On Her Majesty's Secret Service* (1963).

Below: Missing Nazi treasure was also the subject of W Stanley Moss's book. *Gold Is Where You Hide It* (1956).

GOLD IS
WHERE YOU
HIDE IT

W. STANLEY MOSS
Author of ILL-MET BY MOONLIGHT

What happened
to the
Reichsbank Treasure?

2'6

English and
American planes
attacking an Axis
convoy off the
coast of Corsica
in 1943

A contemporary sketch of Bastia after the Allied bombing raids had freed the island from German and Italian occupation.

Left: A German U-boat being attacked by an Allied bomber off Cap Sud, Corsica, in 1943.

Right: Johnny Ramensky, 'The Prince of Safe-Crackers', who turned from criminal to war hero in the search for secret German documents.

Below: La Spezia, the Italian port where the paths of Johnny Ramensky and Peter Fleig crossed . . .

The exotic town of Gabès in Tunisia, where the trail of Rommel's Gold began in 1942.

Sfax, the Tunisian Port where the cargo of looted Nazi valuables sailed off into legend from war-torn North Africa.

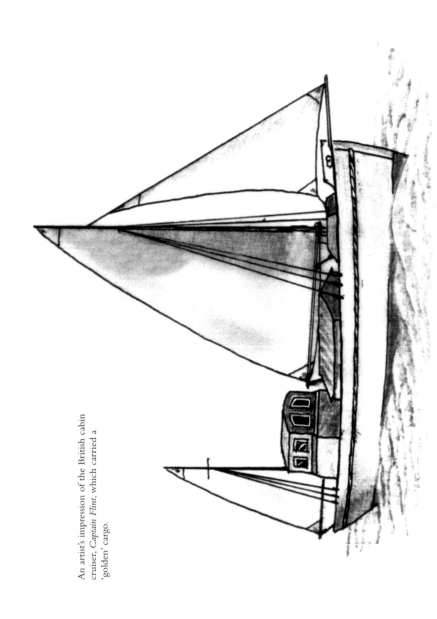

An artist's impression of the British cabin cruiser, *Captain Flint*, which carried a 'golden' cargo.

A trio of German soldiers rescued from the sea off the coast of Corsica in 1943 as the Axis forces were evacuating the island.

Right: 'The Dreamweaver', Ed Link, the famous American underwater explorer, was just one of many people who searched for Rommel's Gold.

Below: Sea Diver, Ed Link's high-tech boat used in his deep-sea explorations in the Mediterranean and Tyrrhenian seas in 1963.

above: Propriano, where the French driver, André Mattei – who claimed to have found the location of Rommel's Gold – was murdered.

below: The Etang de Biguglia, a landlocked stretch of water on the east coast of Corsica, close to the site of the missing Nazi gold.

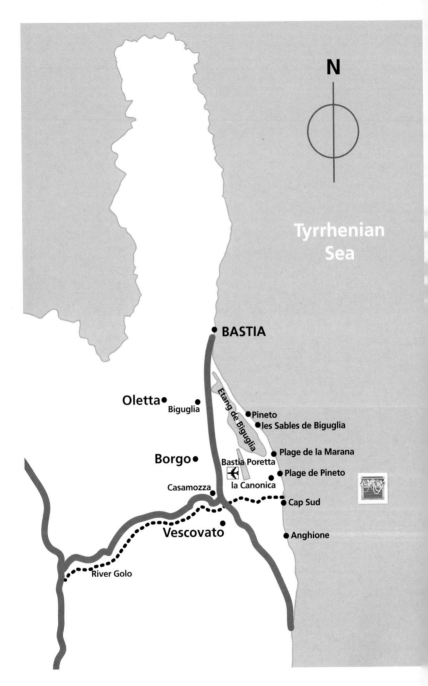

Map of the east coast of Corsica, indicating the position of Rommel's Gold.

particular, the gaunt ruins of Montozone, a town where some Nazi soldiers had been ambushed by partisans and in retaliation the Germans had brought in tanks and laid the entire area to waste.

When La Spezia was in range of binoculars, Lieutenant Crandall found a vantage point on the slopes of Mount Rocchetta to the east of the port. The following day he radioed Major Hawkins with details of the German gun entrenchments. The enemy's first line of defence was machine-gun nests and behind them, hidden in caves in the Apuan Alps, were the big guns. These were mounted on rails and, after firing, could be rolled back into the safety of the tunnels.

Armed with this information, the Allied bombers were now able to launch accurate strikes at the German defences. Alongside them on one raid flew a plane with supplies of fresh food, drink, cigarettes, weapons, ammunition and explosives for the Commandos hiding nearby.

After a week of intensive bombing, the German guns fell silent and the group in the hills felt confident about moving into La Spezia. In the town, one of the partisans, Luigi Valtera, who had accompanied the group all the way from Livorno, asked Johnny for a favour. The Italian knew all about his skill with explosives and wanted him to blow up the headquarters of the local Fascists. It was these traitors, along with the Germans, who had been responsible for so much pain and suffering in this part of Italy, Valtera said. But he was anxious that none of the neighbouring houses where ordinary people lived should be damaged.

It was just the kind of challenge that Johnny Ramensky relished – and after the devastation he had seen at Montozone he was happy to assist in an act of retribution. He asked for a map of the building that stood at the corner of a busy square. It had two storeys: the ground floor was full of offices while the second was a large dormitory for the Fascists and several German officers. Johnny decided he would have to put his explosives about thirty feet above street level for maximum effect.

What he devised from his available store of materials was a bomb consisting of 60lb of plastic explosives in two sandbags fitted with guncotton primers and an instantaneous fuse. A double lead fuse 30 feet long attached to each bag would allow two minutes to get clear.

At 3 a.m., Ramensky and his team installed the bomb. Once again, Johnny had to use all the skills he had developed as a cat burglar to shin up the wall and put the bomb in position against the dormitory window. Then he hurried down and set the fuse.

Two minutes later, as the group sprinted from the square, an explosion ripped off the top of the Fascist headquarters, killing all those inside. Not a soul in any of the adjoining buildings received so much as a scratch – although every occupant was jarred awake by the noise and was soon delightedly discussing what had obviously happened.

For several weeks thereafter, Johnny Ramensky was kept busy sabotaging railway lines and military installations to aid the Allied advance until La Spezia was at last freed. Then it was time to deal with all the captured German and Fascist safes in the town. Under Major Hawkins's instructions, Ramensky cracked more than thirty safes and they spewed forth a host of documents. Some again related to the Germans' secret plans for Italy after the collapse of Mussolini's forces; others detailing the strength and deployment of the military forces in the district.

But a number of other papers found in La Spezia proved even more interesting. These referred specifically to consignments of valuable paintings, jewellery and cash intended for shipment to Germany. Among them was a document referring to a special consignment from North Africa bound for Berlin that had gone terribly astray.

For years afterwards, Johnny Ramensky occasionally recalled the papers he had pulled in great bundles from the safes in La Spezia. Unfortunately, there were so many that he never had a chance to look at any in detail before they were boxed up to be sent back to Intelligence officers in London.

There is, however, evidence that the Prince of Safe-crackers may have seen details of the plunder that became known as Rommel's Gold, the instructions for its transportation, and wondered what had happened to it in all the subsequent chaos and confusion of the Allied advance. Certainly, there are clues to be found in the remaining years of Ramensky's life to support this theory.

The fall of Italy was not long in coming after the Allies had taken La Spezia, and Major Hawkins and his Commandos were soon moved on again as the noose tightened around Nazi Germany. Ramensky spent the rest of the war opening safes belonging to the rapidly disintegrating Third Reich and by all accounts no safe could withstand the 'fineness of the Ramensky touch', to quote one report.

Percy Sillitoe's biographer, A W Cockerill, has some interesting facts to add concerning this period:

Ramensky was fond of telling the story of how he was taken to Berlin to blow open Hitler's safe in the Reichstag. Apparently, the Allies searched in vain for a means of opening the safe without damaging the contents and finally called upon Ramensky to do the job. He agreed to do it, but on condition that he should *perform the task alone* [my italics] and, having been supplied with all the equipment for which he asked, the door was blown open and the contents removed intact.

Johnny never explained *why* he asked to be on his own for this particular job – it had not bothered him to have people around him in his other war work – and the question must remain as to whether he suspected, perhaps even knew, that something really useful to him might be held in the Führer's safe. Even then it was well known that Hitler had spent years gathering a great collection of stolen treasure from all over Europe and details could well have resided in that safe.

A villain Johnny Ramensky may well have been before the war, but he emerged after his three years' service something of a hero. Major Hawkins and his superiors in the British Special Forces were delighted with his contribution to the victory. He was even offered another job – to serve as a secret agent in a displaced persons' camp – but decided he had had enough of Army life and was demobbed on 6 June 1946 with a glowing testimonial.

On his return to Glasgow, Ramensky seemingly tried to resist falling back into a life of crime. He used his discharge money from the Army to open a bookmaker's shop, but within a year it had failed – mainly because of his good nature towards losing punters. And, as one of his friends remarked years later: 'Johnny also played the horses, dogs and cards himself. All his money went that way. As fast as he earned it, he spent it. For a gambler to be a bookmaker was like an alcoholic working in a boozer.'

So Ramensky returned to crime. In 1947, he was caught after blowing a safe in a Glasgow office building and received a five-year sentence – although he got time off for good behaviour and was released in 1950. For a while he lived happily with Lily Mulholland, a widow whom he had known since childhood. But in December of that year, short of money once again, he robbed the Cardonald Post Office in Glasgow, making away with cash and savings stamps valued at £750.

When he was inevitably arrested and appeared at Glasgow High Court, Johnny pleaded guilty for the first time in his life – hoping, as he put it, 'that I might get away with it due to a fault of the law'. But there was no such omission to help him and he was sent down for a five-year sentence at Peterhead jail.

Perhaps with memories of his former wife in mind, Johnny repeated his previous daring escape on 31 July 1953. Quite how he got out of his cell and over the wall this time is still a mystery, but it was not until 46 hours later that he was recaptured – in marshland just a few yards away from where he had been found almost exactly twenty years earlier. This time, however, his explanation that he was homesick for Lily actually impressed the prison governor and his sentence was not increased.

In February 1954 Ramensky was again set free and two weeks later he and Lily were married. For eight months he steered clear of trouble – working in a grocery store – until a bad loss at a greyhound track caused him to break into a laundry and relieve the safe of almost £3,000.

This time Johnny appealed in court for leniency on the grounds of his wartime service. He told the court he had committed the crime in a fit of anger over his gambling loss and referred to 'thirty years of misery and privation' in and out of prison during his 52 years of existence. 'The law has had more than its pound of flesh,' he protested to the magistrate. 'Would it be wrong to ask for a chance now? My resolution to turn away from crime may seem late, but better late than never.'

In fact, it *was* too late for Johnny Ramensky and he was sentenced to ten years preventive detention – despite a last, impassioned appeal by Lily that her husband was not a vicious criminal, but a man who 'craved excitement, who faced temptations others rarely faced and who could never get a real grip on life'.

Johnny may well not have been able to get a grip on life, but he could certainly still get a grip on the walls of Peterhead Prison. During 1958 he broke out of the prison three more times, establishing a record number of escapes worthy of the *Guinness Book of Records*.

The first of these jail-breaks on 31 January was made with the aid of a ladder stolen from a shed in the prison yard and used to get over the wall. He was free for just 24 hours. The second, on 17 October, was achieved by breaking out of a locked recreation room and he was on the run for 48 hours before being recaptured in a barn.

The third – and most remarkable – escape occurred on 16 December when Johnny broke out of the exercise yard in Peterhead in full daylight wearing prison clothing. As the days passed and no sign of him was found, rumours began to circulate that he had drowned in the river or died of exposure.

Then, all of a sudden on Boxing Day, a bedraggled figure was spotted by a lorry driver on the outskirts of Aberdeen, some thirty miles from the jail.

News of Ramensky's recapture made front-page news and was described by the police almost with grudging admiration as 'probably the most remarkable in British prison history'. Over 200 people waited outside the prison to cheer his return, one of them shouting to the handcuffed man, 'Good luck, Gentleman Johnny!'

It was a still bright-eyed, but rather less virile Ramensky who completed his sentence at Peterhead in 1965. The ever-faithful Lily was there waiting for him and the couple disappeared from the limelight for several years. Johnny, however, still had hopes of making enough money for both of them to enjoy a little comfort and perhaps even travel abroad.

Ramensky had, in fact, been telling his friends for years that he dreamed of returning to Italy. He particularly wanted to go back and see Rome where, he said, he had 'my most exciting experience'. Some among those who knew him well believed this referred more to what he had seen among the documents in the safes than to actually blowing them open which was, after all, almost second nature to him.

Then, in 1969, Ramensky was offered just such a chance when he was invited by the British Special Forces to a reunion in Rome to celebrate the 25th anniversary of Commando operations in Italy. British soldiers were to be reunited with the partisans with whom they had shared such desperate and exciting days fighting the Germans. The celebrations included trips to several of the places where the two groups had fought their hardest battles, notably La Spezia. Lily urged Johnny to go.

Although Ramensky was by this time in failing health – he would die just three years later in 1972 – memories must have stirred in his mind as he once again visited the places where he had used his peerless safe-cracking skills to such good effect: in particular the former German Embassy in Rome and the Nazi headquarters in La Spezia.

Reunited with his friend, Luigi Valtera, Johnny spent hours with him reminiscing about their experiences: tramping across the dangerous countryside for days on end, blowing up the Fascist headquarters, and removing the mountains of documents from the opened safes. In La Spezia, Valtera especially remembered Johnny's wistful mention of a document he had seen that referred to 'a treasure trove of gold from North Africa' as he described it. But he said nothing more specific, according to the Italian.

Could this piece of paper have referred in some way to the hoard that became known as Rommel's Gold? It is certainly a possibility, although there is no evidence that Johnny ever thought of trying to recover it. But it is, nonetheless, interesting to speculate that on his return to La Spezia, Johnny Ramensky stood on the hilly area of Manarola where he and Valtera had once gazed down on the port, and pondered in his smart criminal mind a treasure trove beyond the dreams of avarice. He may even have seen through the golden haze settling over the sea the outline of an island, without the slightest idea that the dream was closer than he could have imagined.

Because on that island of Corsica – 80 miles away by a five-hour ferry ride – lay all the clues to the whereabouts of that elusive gold just waiting to be discovered.

7

The Quest of Peter Fleig

If it is impossible to be sure just how closely Johnny Ramensky was involved in the search for Rommel's Gold, the same is certainly not the case with Peter Fleig, a German soldier who served in Italy in 1943. For by this man's own account – confirmed by information obtained from a number of other sources – he actually took part in hiding the loot off the coast of Corsica.

Fleig is, without doubt, the most intriguing and enigmatic figure associated with the legendary hoard. Piecing together the story of his life and his involvement with the six missing cases – not to mention his own attempts to recover the treasure after the war – takes us from Germany to Italy and on to Corsica, with a detour to Russia at probably the bleakest and most bloody period in its history.

The story is, though, complicated by Fleig's elusiveness, his evasiveness about certain details of his activities and occasionally his deliberate omission of facts. What follows in this chapter is as accurate a description of the man and his part in the saga of Rommel's Gold as it has been possible to compile.

Peter Fleig – his surname is occasionally spelt Fleigh – was born on 19 February 1921 in the ancient Czech city of Rumburk, an aptly named place that sticks rather like a clenched fist into the rump of Germany just below Dresden. Part of North Bohemia, the city's only claim to fame is for its inhabitants' role in the military rebellion against the Austro-Hungarian regime in 1918. Its location on the borderland of two uneasy nations has bred a people noted for their reserve – although they also possess considerable determination and, when necessary, a deal of cunning.

Fleig's father was a jeweller by trade, a profession that had flourished in North Bohemia since the late nineteenth century. A taciturn yet rather fiery man, he had survived the First World War, married shortly afterwards and fathered his only child, Peter, a year later. Young Peter Fleig with his blond hair and rather heavy-lidded blue eyes grew up with the sight of gold, silver and precious stones in front of him every day. He was apparently intent on following in his father's footsteps until the rise of Nazism and Hitler's seizure of Czechoslovakia in 1938 swallowed him up into the events of the Second World War.

There are stories that Fleig was something of a loner, given to outbursts of rage, and may even have been in trouble with the police before he signed up for the German Army. According to one version of his life – and Ian Fleming repeats it in *On Her Majesty's Secret Service* – Fleig was recruited into the *Abwehr* (the Foreign Bureau/Defence of the Armed Forces High Command), the German Reich's most important military Intelligence service during the war. There is, however, no evidence to support this claim – though Fleig with his tendency to boast may well have encouraged others to believe the story.

122

Certainly there is no record that he ever served as an *Obersturmführer* (First Lieutenant) as has been claimed.

In fact, Peter Fleig joined the German Army and was trained in Stuttgart as an engineer and fitter. He first saw action in France and after the rapid success of that campaign was transferred, like Rommel who had masterminded it, to North Africa. Based in Libya, Fleig was given an engineering role servicing tanks and equipment for the Afrika Korps. During this period, he also learned deep-sea diving, perfecting his skills in the warm, clear waters of the Mediterranean.

Such halcyon days did not last long, however. Fleig narrowly escaped death during the Germans' bloody retreat across Libya and after a traumatic posting to Italy just prior to the Fascist nation's collapse, served in Hitler's catastrophic campaign in Russia. As luck would have it, Fleig survived this carnage, but was badly injured and sent back home to a hospital in Stuttgart.

Life in that city which had been badly hit by Allied bombing raids was a matter of surviving one day at a time and Peter Fleig was fortunate to receive medical care. By the end of the war he was by all accounts a gaunt and emaciated figure with a large scar down the right side of his face. He suffered badly from headaches and was constantly morose and argumentative.

Little is known about what Fleig did to scratch a living for himself in the city between the years 1945 and 1947. His injuries were such that he had to make frequent returns to hospital for treatment. It is possible that his skill as a fitter got him the occasional job on one of the building sites that dotted the area between the Hauptstatter Strasse and the Jagerstrasse, where builders were hard at work recreating the shattered city from the ground up.

What Peter Fleig *did* do was mull over a secret he had been harbouring for almost five years. And when he decided to try to cash in on this secret, his activities come into much clearer focus.

Stuttgart, like a number of major German cities at this time, contained various consulates representing the victorious Allied nations. In fact, it had three – one British, one American and one French. On a winter day in 1947, Fleig presented himself at the French consulate close to the railway station on Königstrasse and requested an application form for a visa. He wanted to go to Corsica, he told the clerk on duty.

It was an unusual request and one that puzzled the official who was unnerved enough by Peter Fleig's appearance. The man knew that Corsica had remained loyal to France throughout its occupation by 80,000 Italians and 12,000 Germans, including the notorious Gestapo. It had taken the unremitting efforts of 12,000 patriots supplied with arms by the Allies to finally liberate the country on 4 October 1943 – the first department of France to be set free.

Not surprisingly, the Corsicans now nursed a deep hatred of anything or anyone German. Indeed, at that time the only Germans on the island were prisoners of war desperate to get *out*. There would hardly be a welcome awaiting a casual German visitor, the man explained, and it would probably be risky even to go there. He asked Fleig to come back the following day to discuss the purpose of his visit in detail.

The next morning, the scarred ex-soldier found himself seated opposite the Consul himself. Thereafter followed a lengthy interrogation during which Fleig was informed in no uncertain manner that he would certainly not get permission unless he admitted the real reason he wanted to go to Corsica. Peter Fleig apparently sighed resignedly and came clean.

For the next two hours the incredulous French Consul listened to a tale of buried gold that Fleig claimed lay under the sea off the Corsican coast – the location of which only he knew. The reason he wanted the visa was to go back to the island and find the treasure.

The story may well have sounded to the Consul like a piece of fiction from an overheated imagination. But despite Fleig's dishevelled appearance and scarred features, the Frenchman believed him. Fleig's claim would be investigated, he said, but strictly under French control.

From a summary of this interview plus evidence gathered later in Corsica from local inhabitants and by several French newspapers including *Le Monde*, *Paris-Press*, *L'Intransigeant* and the populist *L'Espoir de Nice*, not forgetting the investigations of two journalists, Jean Caubet and Charles Van Deusen, it is possible to retell Peter Fleig's story and his part in launching the first post-war hunt for Rommel's Gold.

Fleig's extraordinary tale begins in Italy in the summer of 1943. Following the débâcle of the Afrika Korps in North Africa and Field Marshal Rommel's summons back to Germany, Fleig and several other Army personnel with diving experience were assigned to new duties at La Spezia in July.

The port, as a vital link in the supply route for the German and Italian war efforts, provided plenty of work for deep-sea divers in keeping the area operational. Among their tasks were checking for mines that might have been attached to Axis shipping by the local resistance fighters and helping in the rescue of the pilots and crews of Luftwaffe planes brought down in the Ligurian Sea by Allied aircraft.

The Allies were already making good use of their new position of strength in North Africa. They were on the verge of retaking Sicily from the Italians and would soon turn their attention to capturing Italy itself. Allied aircraft would then be in an ideal position to do real damage to the German supply lines in this particular theatre of war.

Fleig, though, was happy to be working in the sea again after the burning heat of Libya. Each day his diving grew more proficient and he had more spare time than he had ever enjoyed in the cauldron of North Africa. There were also dark-eyed, voluptuous Italian women in La Spezia happy to help him spend his money in the bustling waterfront cafés and bars.

Even with the crisis looming on the horizon, Peter Fleig made the most of the month of August. Then, on 16 September, he received new orders. He was to travel immediately to the port of Bastia in Corsica taking a complete deep-sea diving outfit and half a dozen air bottles. The order was signed by *Hauptman* Ludwig Dahl.

A fast Italian speedboat picked him up from La Spezia harbour that evening and set off on a direct route across the 80 miles of sea to Corsica. Fleig's mind was full of questions about what his job might be as the boat chopped through the spray towards the island. The line in his orders that had puzzled him the most stated blandly that his diving equipment was to be destroyed 'once the mission has been accomplished'.

A German Army officer was awaiting the boat in Bastia harbour and immediately hustled Peter Fleig and his equipment into a covered lorry. He was driven through the streets of the town and, just as a clock struck midnight, the lorry turned into the courtyard of an imposing building with bowed windows that he would later learn was the Marboeuf Barracks.

Inside the echoing, dimly lit building three other men were waiting. Even in the poor light, Fleig could see that they were all officers. One of the men stepped forward and raised his arm in the traditional 'Heil Hitler' salute. Fleig responded nervously as his eyes met those of the other man.

The officer introduced himself as Captain Ludwig Dahl who had given the order to summon him to Corsica. He was in charge of a special commando unit entrusted with a most important mission. Fleig would follow all his commands without question, he boomed.

Peter Fleig felt his mouth go dry and he swallowed hard. 'Of course, Herr Hauptman,' was all he could think to say, his mind a fever of emotions. Later, he would learn that the three other men, Gunther Cranz, Hans Schaub and Albert Hoffmeyer, were all lieutenants.

Fleig now takes up the story himself in a statement he later gave to a French journalist from *L'Espoir de Nice*. The account may well be laced with a little fantasy, but is believed to be essentially true.

A few hours after my arrival in Bastia, I was ordered to board a motor launch which put out to sea at once. As we reached a particular position some way from the shore, I was told to put on my diving kit and dive. The officer told me I was to look out for a particularly unusual rock formation.

It took me some time to find the position which was at a depth of about 80 metres. When I told Captain Dahl, he marked the co-ordinates on a sea chart and we returned to Bastia.

If these events left Peter Fleig somewhat mystified, stranger things still were to follow. Within minutes of returning, he told the French journalist, he found himself gazing dumbfounded at the most fabulous treasure he had ever seen.

> As soon as I arrived back in Bastia, I was put into another large room in the Marboeuf Barracks. There I watched two of the lieutenants weld up six lead and tin crates of valuables. They were full of bars of gold, silver chalices, little religious caskets set with precious stones, diamonds, jewellery, pearls and a number of paintings. When the crates were all sealed, they were loaded on to a lorry and taken to the same boat we had gone to sea in earlier.*

Understandably filled with curiosity, Peter Fleig spent the rest of his time with the four men piecing together the story of the mysterious cases, their origin and ultimate destination. It was treasure fit for a king, he hardly needed telling. It had to be worth millions, perhaps billions of Reichmarks.

Subsequently, Fleig was to put various figures on the value of the six chests, depending on whom he was speaking to and his state of inebriation. These figures varied from £30 million at the lower end of the scale to over a $100 million at the top.

---

* Although Peter Fleig was no art expert, he later claimed that several of the canvases were the works of famous Italian Renaissance painters and he believed that among the others were pictures by Rembrandt, Chagall and Picasso, all of which seems highly unlikely.

From Captain Dahl himself Fleig learned that the valuables had come from North Africa and were destined for Berlin. They were believed to be a gift for the Führer himself. It would not be until much later that he would discover the cache had been taken from wealthy Jewish families in Tunisia. Nor that it would become known as Rommel's Gold.

The six cases had been transported by ship from Sfax to Naples, where Dahl and his men had taken charge. The Captain's original orders were to transport the cases by road through northern Italy and then across occupied Austria to Germany. However, the plan ran into trouble almost from the start. British and American bombers were now attacking the main Italian roads and railways leading north and, to make matters worse, the partisans were also ambushing lorries and trucks and stealing their contents.

By the time Captain Dahl reached Rome, his orders were changed. The unit were to re-route by sea to Corsica. There they would join a convoy bound for La Spezia and recommence the overland journey to Germany.

This explanation only served to mystify Peter Fleig still more. If it was intended to get the six cases to Berlin, what on earth had he been doing diving off the coast of Bastia looking for an unusual rock formation?

It was Lieutenant Hans Schaub who filled him in on this part of the jigsaw puzzle. Two days earlier on the morning of 15 September, as their boat had been nearing Corsica, the unit's whole mission had suddenly been jeopardised. Just as the vessel was passing the estuary of the River Golo, two American fighter planes had attacked. The planes were evidently part of a larger formation of enemy aircraft heading in the direction of Bastia and clearly intent on attacking a German convoy being assembled there.

Mercifully, the attack on them had only been brief, Schaub said. The strafing by the planes' machine guns had not seriously damaged the motor launch and a bomb aimed at the craft had missed completely. Captain Dahl had quickly sought the safety of the Corsican coast to decide on his next course of action.

His options were not good. If they stayed where they were and the fighter aircraft came back they would be a sitting target and their precious cargo lost for ever. If they travelled up the thirteen miles of coast to Bastia, there was a possibility that the enemy action there might make it impossible to reach La Spezia. Worst of all, there was the risk that the Führer's treasure might fall into enemy hands whatever move they made. And if that happened, neither he nor his men required any imagination to guess what their fate would be.

In the end, Captain Dahl, the dedicated soldier and loyal Nazi, felt it was his unshakable duty to save the six cases at all costs. According to Schaub, he decided the only solution was to hide them in the sea as soon as possible and return for them later when things had returned to normal. After all, the Führer was promising the German people a secret weapon that would soon enable the forces of the Third Reich to win a great victory.

Once Dahl had made his decision, the four men sailed immediately for Bastia. On arriving at a scene of damaged buildings and wrecked equipment, they were initially dismayed to find the convoy had left, but learned that another was being hastily assembled.

There was time, therefore, for Captain Dahl to activate his plan. As none of his men were divers, he dispatched an order for an experienced sub-aqua soldier to be sent from La Spezia. He had no intention of using anyone on the island who would then be left behind with knowledge of the hiding place. The diver who carried out the mission, Peter Fleig, has filled in the details of what happened next, as quoted in *L'Espoir de Nice*:

> On the morning of 18 September we set out in the boat and reached the position we had marked the previous day. I was ordered to dive down to the rock formation. I signalled to the officers when I found it and they seemed very pleased.
>
> I then had to go down with each of the cases as they were put over the side of the launch. The cavity where they rested was marked with four weighted buoys. Without these it would have been impossible to locate the position again.

Unbeknown to the others, however, Peter Fleig was fixing the position of the cases in his own mind, too. He was later to claim that this was about four and a half kilometres offshore at a location where the water was between 116 and 136 feet deep. The seabed itself, he said, was mainly sandy with occasional rocky patches. *Location*

Fleig was also to maintain that he noticed two lights on the coast – one red and one white – which lay in a direct line with the boat and served him as another marker. These lights are the subject of argument, as we shall see.

What is beyond doubt is that Peter Fleig was an exhausted man by the time he had fixed the last of the buoys to the chests with thirty feet of cable. As he swam back to the surface using the last of his air supply, his final memory was of the buoys suspended like sentinels in the gloom.

Even before he was back on board the boat again, though, Peter Fleig had made up his mind about one thing. If things didn't work out as planned, he was intending to come back one day to claim the fortune for himself.

The rest of Peter Fleig's story lacks some of the high adventure of the first part, but is not without its dramas. Another statement by him describes the next turn of events. 'After the six cases had been put on the seabed, there was a long discussion among the four officers. Some wanted to stay in Bastia and get a passage on the convoy. The others wanted to go directly to La Spezia. Eventually La Spezia got the vote. Remarkably, considering the Allied attacks which were going on around Corsica, we made the journey safely and got there on the afternoon of 18 September.'

No mention of the hiding of the six cases was made among the men until they reached the Italian port. There Dahl presented himself to the German Commandant and filed a report of his actions, a copy of which was promptly forwarded to Berlin. The Captain believed he had taken the right decision by hiding the treasure.

Fleig, however, had no time to debate the rights and wrongs of the officer's action. 'Soon after I arrived in La Spezia, I was taken in another covered lorry to a property just outside the town. There I was interrogated by the SS about what had happened. Although I told them exactly what had happened, I was beaten until I was unconscious. I knew nothing of what was going on elsewhere for a whole month.'

In the interim, it transpired, Dahl's decision had been relayed to Hitler – or more likely senior officers in the Reich

Chancellery – and it caused outrage. His orders had been specifically to ensure the safe delivery of the six cases and this he had failed to do. One rumour that has never been substantiated maintains that Hitler flew into one of his rages when he was informed that the treasure from Tunisia had been left in waters that would soon be under Allied control. Now the pictures in the cases would never find a place in the Führermuseum. Certainly, the instructions that were telegraphed from Germany back to northern Italy made no mention of the Iron Cross that Dahl might have secretly hoped for. Instead, he and his three officers were to be court-martialled.

At the military court that was subsequently convened at Massa some twenty miles down the coast from La Spezia, the prosecuting officer accused Dahl and his men of ignoring their instructions in order to steal the priceless treasure for themselves. Counsel asked the presiding judge to sentence the men to death for disobeying instructions and betraying military secrets. Their execution, he said, should serve as a warning to all others who might be tempted to covet riches destined for the Führer. The *Gruppenführer* (Major-General) took just five minutes to order all four to die by firing squad.

Fleig knew nothing of these events in his cell. 'I was kept in isolation for a whole month,' he said in his last statement, 'and then against my wishes I was sent to a unit in Russia. I learned later that the German officers who had taken part in the operation had been shot. They had exonerated me during their interrogation by stating that I was just a soldier who had been carrying out orders to the best of my ability. They saved my life.'

Whatever gratitude Peter Fleig may have felt then did not last long. Before Christmas, he found himself in the freezing hell of Russia serving in the German Eighth Army on the Ukrainian front.

The details of Fleig's service record at this time are unclear, as Jean Caubet, a freelance Corsican journalist who wrote several articles on the story for French periodicals, discovered while making enquiries. One piece of evidence suggested he was wounded and taken prisoner by the Russians. Another version claimed he was shot in the head during hand-to-hand fighting in the Ukraine which left him with the scar on his face.

It seems more likely that he was one of the lucky soldiers to have escaped the fate that overwhelmed the Eighth Army when ten of its divisions were trapped by the Russian General Koniev's troops south-east of Kiev in a battle that lasted for fourteen days in February 1944. This battle was said to have been the biggest of its kind since the destruction of the German Sixth Army at Stalingrad. Certainly, it prompted a typical rousing propaganda speech by Stalin that the enemy had 'abandoned 52,000 killed on the battlefield, leaving all their equipment and armour to be captured along with 11,000 prisoners'.

Many exhausted and frozen German soldiers had, in fact, surrendered despite an order from Hitler instructing them to 'commit suicide if the position became hopeless'. If escaping from such a situation seems improbable even for a man like Peter Fleig, it is also true to say that probably only someone with his luck would have been able to do so.

Whatever the truth, Fleig was certainly back in Stuttgart in 1945 when the Third Reich collapsed. He required regular medical attention and claimed that the one thing that kept him going was the dream of returning to Corsica and claiming the fortune that lay off the estuary of the River Golo.

Fleig knew that all the others involved in hiding the treasure were dead. The four officers had been shot and that surely made him the only person who knew the exact location of the six chests. What he did not know was that someone else had actually seen the disposal of the loot.

The eyewitness was a Frenchman named Louis Bordes who happened to be on the coast of Corsica that same morning in 1943. The event stayed fixed in his mind as an oddity at a time when the island was wracked by upheaval.

Bordes was to describe later how the Germans and Italians were busy evacuating the island as fast as they could with the tide of war turning rapidly against them. The local resistance fighters had been waiting for this moment and were harassing the enemy at every opportunity – especially around Bastia. With Allied planes attacking daily, the local Maquis, the underground resistance movement named after the brush country of Corsica, struck wherever confusion among the enemy was at its greatest. Louis Bordes had been an active participant in this struggle for freedom for some months, as he told a reporter of *L'Intransigeant*:

On the night of 17–18 September 1943 I was in the village of Poreta on the gulf of Bastia with a group of Corsican partisans. I was near the coast with my field glasses. During the early morning greyness I suddenly saw a small boat with no flag.

Being curious about what it was doing in the bay, I climbed onto a rock to be able to see better. As I looked through my glasses I saw several men putting six large cases overboard.

Louis Bordes had no time for further investigation. The partisans moved along the coast towards Bastia where the sound of explosions and the sight of leaping flames amid the ships in the harbour indicated that the local uprising – and the imminent arrival of a Free French task force – would soon set the island free once more. But his memory of the men on the boat would not go away. There seemed to be no reason he could think of for anyone to be dumping cases in the sea unless they were the enemy. Perhaps Italian, but more likely German? It was not until he later heard the first rumours of the missing treasure from North Africa that Bordes felt he might have a solution to the mystery.

Peter Fleig was, of course, quite unaware that he and the others had been observed – albeit that the eyewitness would not appreciate the significance of what he had seen for some years. By late 1947, Fleig's health had improved to the extent that he began to plan an expedition to recover the treasure.

First, he made contact with another diver, also a Czech, Heinz Binder, with whom he had served during the war and together they made preparations to return to Corsica. The only problem was getting a visa – and this resulted in the fateful meeting with the French Consul at which Peter Fleig was forced to reveal his intentions as well as abandoning any plans of a joint venture with Binder.

According to Charles Van Deusen, an American feature writer for several US magazines including *Life* and *True Magazine*, the French government reacted to Fleig's story 'as though it had been stung'. He continues: 'Then after collecting itself and checking over the facts as well as it could, it decided to take over. A sum of $3,000 was allocated to the job and a search party, including the reluctant Fleig, was assembled.'

French Gov't

The party arrived at Bastia in the summer of 1948. The French government had put in charge an experienced marine salvage operator named Rudolf Loebenberg from Bremen whose ship was well equipped with diving facilities, cranes and winches. The plan was for Fleig to dive again in the spot where he had last seen the treasure and use the equipment to haul the loot to the surface.

It was impossible for the arrival of a salvage ship to go unnoticed in Bastia and it was not long before rumours about 'Rommel's Gold' – as the treasure was now being called – were common gossip in the waterfront bars and cafés. A few locals claimed to have known about the story for years, others that the location was actually close to the port off the sand bar known as the Etang de Biguglia.

In one version of the story, the ship used by the Germans had actually been much bigger than a motor launch and had travelled from the Italian coast with two lorries containing the valuables on board. One of these was loaded with works of art and the other with six crates, each weighing 600kg. Five were packed with 2,400 bars of gold, all apparently 'stamped with the Ethiopian lion', and the sixth with jewellery and precious stones.

This particular rumour claimed that when the boat ran into trouble with the aircraft off the besieged coast of Corsica, the Germans had panicked and decided to get rid of the heavy booty in order not to slow down their escape. They had tipped the lorry containing the works of art into the estuary of the River Golo and dropped the second holding the cases of gold further out to sea. While this account is generally discredited, what is certain is that no one knew the 'area of probability' in which the treasure lay better than Peter Fleig.

Jean Caubet says the expedition spent two months diving in the area of the Golo estuary. During this time, Fleig apparently told Rudolf Loebenberg that he had seen red and white lights on the coast that had helped him to mark the spot. Now they were no longer there.

Loebenberg puzzled over this fact for some time, wondering how lights could have been visible in daylight. He discovered, that there were two red beacons in use on the airport at Poreta in September 1943 – but what about the white light? After visiting the location by day and night and realising it was possible to see the lights only in darkness, Loebenberg began to suspect that the ex-soldier might be deliberately trying to avoid finding the treasure.

Prompted by his suspicions, the salvage expert sent down two of his own divers to explore the same area – yet still nothing came to light. Charles Van Deusen takes up the story again: 'Then bad weather set in and everyone agreed that the best thing to do was to resume activities the following summer.'

Jean Caubet, for his part, was sure about the real reason for this lack of success, as he wrote in *L'Espoir de Nice*.

When Fleig first approached the French consul in Stuttgart he was hoping for the equivalent of a million francs for his secret. All they were paying him while he dived was five hundred francs a day with no promise of a share in the proceeds when the treasure was found. So suppose he did spot the chests, but concealed the fact with the intention of coming back another time to get them for himself? *That's* what some people on Corsica think.

Whatever the truth, events conspired to wreck the French plan.

The records of the Bastia police office state that in September 1948, a charge of stealing a camera was brought by Rudolf Loebenberg against Peter Fleig. The case came before the local magistrates' court at the end of that month. The investigating officer, André Sanguinetti, told the justice that Fleig had disposed of the camera in a local bar to obtain drinking money. Although Peter Fleig protested his innocence, the magistrate – a man with no love for Germans – sentenced him to two months in jail.

Caubet returns to the story:

While he was in prison, Fleig tried to bribe other prisoners and even some of the guards with little maps he drew of where the treasure was supposed to be, in return for cigarettes, extra food and little privileges. These drawings on scraps of paper and the back of cigarette packets were all contradictory, of course, and it was no surprise that Fleig disappeared the moment he was released. Before then, Loebenberg had run out of patience and funds and packed up his ship and left for Bremen in disgust.

As Charles Van Deusen was to discover, this was not the last to be heard of Peter Fleig. His name would occur again when some very sinister people became involved in the search for Rommel's Gold, the same people – among others – that Ian Fleming had told me about when we talked in his London office.

In the meantime, interest in the legend had grown considerably as a result of the French expedition and the international publicity it had generated. Indeed, the events in Corsica were hardly off the pages of the newspapers before an extraordinary discovery was made thousands of miles away in London at the curiously named Eel Pie Island on the River Thames. It was a discovery that would introduce a completely new element to the mystery of Rommel's Gold.

8

The *Captain Flint*'s Golden Cargo

It was a bitterly cold January morning in 1949 and Eel Pie Island was still and almost completely silent. The little stretch of land just 600 metres long situated in a bend of the River Thames at Twickenham appeared at first glance to have gone into hibernation since the end of its residents' traditionally high-spirited Christmas and New Year parties.

Even the trees ringing it and draping their branches into the water's edge looked for all the world as if they were guarding its tranquillity from inquisitive eyes. In fact, there was no sign of life on either the island or the single metal footbridge that linked it to the outside world.

Eel Pie Island has long been a sanctuary for individuals and eccentrics. Originally named after the eel pie so coveted by Henry VIII that he insisted on having the first pie of each season delivered to Hampton Court by a Twickenham waterman, its colourful history has also included periods as a duelling square, a bowling green and a parade ground for the Duke of York and his troops. Charles Dickens was one of its famous residents from 1855 to 1857 while he wrote *Little Dorrit*, and the place saw its fair share of scandal as the hideaway of the mistresses of a number of leaders of Victorian society. By the time of the Second World War it was established as the last Bohemian outpost in Greater London.

The appearance of Eel Pie Island in 1949 was very much in keeping with the diversity of people who had lived there over the years. Architect-designed houses rubbed shoulders with shanty dwellings, along with a number of varicoloured houseboats moored at numerous points around the water's edge.

There was, though, nothing particularly colourful about the island on that overcast January morning. Across the water in Twickenham, traffic was moving along King Street, York Street and Richmond Road, while a steady flow of people went in and out of the municipal offices on Riverside.

Over the years, Eel Pie Island has sustained various, often esoteric, professions – from portrait painters to guitar makers – but boat building has remained the main 'industry'. Among the best-known ship chandlers have been the Lion Boat Yard, Sim's Yard, and Messum's, the owners of the Viking Yard.

It was in the Viking Yard on this particular morning that the only activity to disturb the general inertia was taking place. A man and a teenage boy were laboriously breaking up an old boat.

The activity was nothing unusual in itself. Vessels of all shapes and sizes that had outlived their usefulness were regularly brought to the island by their owners and sold for salvage. In most cases, the only value in these hulks lay in the fittings that had survived from a more prosperous age – gold and silver furnishings that were still marketable.

The boat being salvaged was a small cabin cruiser with the name *Captain Flint* painted on its bows. It was dank and musty

142

and waterlogged. The boy, at work in the hold removing metal fastenings with the aid of a claw hammer, was already up to the ankles of his Wellington boots in evil-smelling water. As one section of woodwork fell away in his hands he stopped and let out a yell.

'Hey, come and look at this...'

'What?' grunted the older man halfway through unscrewing some fittings in the cruiser's wheelhouse.

'Come and see what I've found,' the teenager shouted again, more insistently.

With a sigh, the man put down his screwdriver and stepped into the hold.

'Christ!' he swore as water splashed over his boots. 'What are you on about?"

The boy said nothing, but pointed urgently into the darkened cavity he had just exposed. When the man's eyes had become accustomed to the gloom, he let out a gasp of surprise.

For lying there, glinting dully but quite unmistakable, was a single gold ingot. Yet, as the two workers looked at one another in silent astonishment, they could hardly have imagined that they had uncovered a link to one of the Second World War's most mysterious treasures.

Over the years, there have been a number of stories about smugglers from abroad using the banks of the River Thames to land their illegal cargoes, even as far upstream as Richmond and Twickenham. Indeed, the police files of the two districts record any number of such incidents, several of which occurred during the immediate post-war years. There is, though, no indication of a boat so aptly named as the *Captain Flint* (after the pirate whose treasure is sought in Robert Louis Stevenson's novel, *Treasure Island*) being involved in any such activities.

The discovery of the gold bar in the vessel did initially raise this kind of speculation, but then it proved to be the first step in a treasure hunt that would lead from London to the south coast of England and thereafter to the Adriatic and the Mediterranean. The trail began in a local newspaper report and was later taken up by a very determined radio journalist who would finally solve the puzzle.

According to the *Twickenham & Whitton Chronicle* which first reported the discovery of the ingot on the *Captain Flint*, the boat was a ketch-rigged cabin cruiser which in its heyday before the war had probably looked rather splendid in its red, white and black paintwork. Powered by a six-cylinder, 30hp Leyland diesel engine fed by rough-weather fuel tanks, it had a range of almost 1,000km as well as an auxiliary fuel tank that could be kept topped up in case of emergencies.

In its central wheelhouse, the *Flint* was controlled by wheel-and-chain steering and guided by a compass and clock mounted in brass. Below decks there was a narrow, four-berth cabin and galley, fitted with a Calor gas cooker and an auxiliary generating plant for the electric lighting.

In addition, the vessel carried two substantial fresh water tanks for long-range cruising and stowed in a locker were three large red sails that could, if necessary, be used as an auxiliary form of propulsion. The polished oak of the bulkhead and the cruiser's sturdy coppered bottom bore witness to the many hundreds of hours of sailing the craft had undertaken during its half century in the water. It was true to say that even in its death throes in the Viking Yard on Eel Pie

Island, it was still possible to see what a fine boat the *Captain Flint* had once been.

From its enquiries, the *Twickenham & Whitton Chronicle* learned that the boat had been sold to the salvagers by Gerry Diamont, manager of the Richmond Ice Skating Rink, who had kept it moored on the Thames by the piles of the rink. He had decided to get rid of the cruiser – which had originally belonged to his father-in-law – after it had fallen into disrepair at its moorings. The *Captain Flint*'s passage to this sad demise had been a circuitous one, the paper reported:

> The boat originally belonged to a Mr Martineau of Hove, Sussex, who was cruising in the Adriatic off Yugoslavia when the war broke out. He left the *Captain Flint* in the care of a boat builder and flew back to England to join the Navy. He was killed at Dunkirk.

Nothing more was heard about the cruiser until 1946 when it turned up over 600 miles away in Corsica.

> British ownership was proved and Anne Martineau, the daughter of the late Lieutenant Martineau, sailed the *Captain Flint* back to England with the help of her fiancé, Gerry Diamont, whom she later married. Sometime later the boat became waterlogged and foundered. The Diamonts sold her to Messum's to defray the cost of salvage.

The event would, in all probability, have gone completely unnoticed if not for the discovery of the gold ingot. Perhaps the account in the *Twickenham & Whitton Chronicle* would also have soon been forgotten had it not been read by a BBC journalist, Peter Eton, who was immediately fascinated by the implications of the find and set about trying to unravel the mystery. His researches provide an extraordinary explanation for the *Captain Flint*'s strange cargo.

George Martineau, the original owner of the cabin cruiser, was a wealthy garage proprietor who had built up a chain of garages along the south coast. From childhood, he had loved tinkering with engines, and although he made his fortune with motor car engines, was at his happiest when sailing boats.

Over the years, Martineau had owned several small craft – including a sea-going yacht which he twice raced during Cowes Week – before purchasing the *Captain Flint*. His horizons were growing wider by then and he made plans to spend his summers sailing in the Atlantic, the Mediterranean and even in the far distant Adriatic. He had already made several successful long voyages around the coast of Europe before he set off for Yugoslavia in the fateful summer of 1939.

The voyage of the cabin cruiser as it passed around the coasts of France, Portugal and Spain and on into the Mediterranean proved idyllic for Martineau, although the news of impending disaster in Europe which came over his radio each day hung like an increasingly dark cloud as he passed Sardinia, Sicily and the toe of Italy before entering the Adriatic.

Martineau hoped against hope that British Prime Minister Chamberlain's assurances of 'peace in our time' would prove correct, but by the time he was in sight of the coast of Yugoslavia he was beginning to have very real doubts. And as he steered between the pretty archipelago of islands that lie between the

Adriatic and the port of Zadar on the last day of August, these doubts became reality.

Three days later, on 3 September, George Martineau heard the declaration of war against Germany and at once changed his plans. He would fly back to England and offer his services to his country. The *Twickenham & Whitton Chronicle* fills in the next piece of the story with moving brevity: 'Martineau was cruising in the Adriatic when war broke out. He left the *Captain Flint* in the care of a boat builder on the Yugoslavian coast and flew back to England to join the Navy. He was killed at Dunkirk.'

There the trail might well have gone cold but for the persistence of Peter Eton, who visited Corsica in June 1946. It was a nostalgic trip for Eton who, as a boy of twelve, had attended the Lycée in Bastia under a school exchange scheme. Now, aged thirty, and just invalided out of the Navy, he was anxious to see how things had changed. Thanks to this and subsequent trips to Corsica he found out a great deal more about the fate of Martineau's boat. Writing some years later in *Conspiracy of Silence*, he explained:

The head of my department, Laurence Gilliam, suggested that as I had a month's holiday coming up I should take a new midget American portable tape recorder, which was on loan to the BBC, on holiday with me to France and record first-hand impressions of the problems of post-war rehabilitation. Once in France, with the wartime prestige of the BBC behind me, I believed I could wangle a visit to my favourite holiday spot – Corsica – although the island was still closed officially to everyone save Corsicans returning from the war and important officials.

During his subsequent stay in Bastia, which was still recovering from the damage inflicted by Allied bombing raids during the occupation, Eton was reunited with Antoine Nicolai, an old friend from his days at the Lycée. The Corsican was now a fisherman making his living catching lobsters and mullet and occasionally renting his boat to visitors. According to Eton, during the war he had not been above the occasional smuggling assignation with boats from Italy ferrying cigarettes, penicillin and illegal drugs.

While on his conducted tours with Nicolai, Eton saw groups of German POWs being put to work restoring what they had helped to destroy. In the cafés and bars the two men frequented, he was also able to pick up the everyday gossip.

In one bar in the harbour area he was introduced to Jakov Jovanovic, a Yugoslav working for the International Allied Reparations Commission based in Brussels. The organisation was charged with tracing loot stolen by the Nazis from churches, museums and Jewish families and returning these valuables to their original owners.

In the course of their very first conversation, Jovanovic excited Eton's journalistic instincts by telling him that there were a number of hoards of stolen treasure buried at various spots in Europe. Eton committed his impressions to paper immediately afterwards: 'Two days ago I had been interviewing an elderly colonel about budgerigars in the bar of The Rose Revived, a riverside inn near Oxford, and now here I was on the quayside of a sultry Mediterranean seaport talking to a mysterious Yugoslav about gold bullion. It was all a bit like a dream, but I decided that the man's story might be true and I wanted to find out more.'

The mysterious Jovanovic turned out to have been an art dealer in Zagreb before the war. He had escaped to England in 1941, served in the Army, and at the end of hostilities joined the Reparations Commission. After a period of training in Brussels he had been assigned to a case in his native country at the request of M Zujovic, the Yugoslavian Minister of Finance who, by a curious coincidence, had been at school with him.

Jovanovic's mission was to discover what had happened to a fortune in bullion belonging to the Société Générale Banquière de Yugoslavie in Zagreb which had disappeared at the time of the country's invasion by the Germans. The bank, a private concern run by Austrians and holding some of King Peter's personal fortune as well as the funds of a number of wealthy local farmers and landowners, had ceased to exist after the Nazi occupation and all its records had been destroyed.

Several weeks into his investigations, Jovanovic had a stroke of luck when an orderly from the hospital of Sveti Duh came to his office. The man had a startling tale to tell him about a patient who had been a messenger for the Société Générale bank and knew all about the missing bullion.

On 9 April 1941, with the country on the verge of collapse in the face of the advancing Germans, the man had been given the job of assistant driver on a truck taking the bank's bullion reserves in wooden boxes to Sarajevo, then still under the control of the Yugoslav provisional government. There it was to be sent out of the country before it could be seized by the enemy.

The truck was accompanied by an escort of two motorcycle outriders and after following a tortuous route along primitive, potholed roads via Karlovak, Bihac, and into the mountain range of the Mala Kapela, it had suddenly run into a German Army scout car near the village of Susevic. The vehicle was a bulky 222 Leichter *Panzerspahwagen* of the 132nd Recce Battalion armed with a 20mm automatic gun and carrying a crew of four.

Perhaps suspicious of the escorts, the scout car had immediately opened fire and killed the two motorcyclists and the driver of the truck. The assistant driver was left apparently dead at the roadside. On investigating the truck, the German soldiers found to their amazement that they had stumbled on a fortune – one estimate put the number of gold bars in it at over three hundred – and the four men quickly loaded the wooden boxes into their scout car and disappeared into the night.

According to Jovanovic's informant, the assistant driver had been lucky to survive. The wrecked truck was found by partisans harrying the advancing Germans, and the man – more dead than alive – was put on a lorry going back north to Zagreb. He survived the journey, recovered slowly from his wounds, and then began to wonder exactly what had happened during and after the ambush.

Jovanovic explained to Eton: 'It was three months before the man was well enough to take the orderly back to the scene of the hold-up. All they could find were the remains of a burnt-out lorry, red with rust, the holes of the German bullets still visible in the bonnet and along the side. That was in July 1941. When the orderly took me there a month ago, the burnt-out vehicle had disappeared. There was nothing but a crude military grave.'

For his part, the Yugoslav said he did not know what to make of the story. The orderly told him the patient claimed there had been roughly 200 million dinars in the boxes – valued at about £1 million at the time – but what had happened to it after it had been snatched by the Germans was a mystery.

The trail of clues had, though, led him to Corsica and Bastia in particular, Jovanovic added – but that was all he was prepared to tell Peter Eton. He was going back to Brussels to report his findings and would leave the Commission to arrange for the recovery of the gold bullion.

Eton himself returned to London shortly afterwards, frustrated that he could extract nothing further from Jakov Jovanovic. He did, though, have the facts of the man's extraordinary story checked out by Tom Waldron, another journalist at the BBC, who could find no discrepancies in the details about the bank, the bullion or how it had been lost.

Then the demands of two new programmes to which Peter Eton was assigned – *Picture Parade* and *The Undefeated* – pushed all thoughts of the missing gold out of his mind. It would take a sudden and inexplicable death to bring the memories flooding back and inspire him to return to Corsica once again to find an answer to the mystery.

Eton was travelling from London to Bristol on the morning of 28 September 1947 to record an episode of *Country Serenade*, a BBC radio programme which investigated the songs and folklore of English counties. As he casually leafed through a copy of the *Daily Telegraph*, a name in a paragraph of a story jumped off the page at him and turned upside down what he had hoped would be a tranquil day. As he recalled later in his book:

The article was dealing with post-war unrest in Europe, in particular how Resistance training had unleashed on the world hundreds of potential murderers. Paris, Marseilles, Nice and Aix seemed to have very bad records, with old scores being paid off between ex-Resistance men and alleged collaborators. But in Lyons there was only one important unsolved murder outstanding – the police had been unable to discover how the body of Mr Jakov Jovanovic, a Yugoslavian official of the Reparations Distribution Commission, came to be found in a backwater of the Rhône.

For the rest of that day – and several more afterwards – Peter Eton found himself going over and over in his mind his conversations with Jovanovic, hoping to find any clue that might throw light on the Yugoslav's death. Could it have had anything to do with the missing gold? That certainly seemed likely – and if so, might well open up a veritable Pandora's box of conspiracy theories as to who the killer, or killers, could have been.

Of one thing, though, there was no doubt. If Jovanovic had been certain the bullion was now in Corsica, it could only have got there from the other side of the Adriatic one way – by boat. But why, he kept asking himself, would anyone want to ship gold to Corsica with the war raging around them?

The pressure of work once again forced Eton to let the mystery slip to the back of his mind, although in the summer of the following year he found himself reminded of it while producing a programme about the discovery of buried treasure. *The Mildenhall Hoard* concerned the discovery by a farm ploughman, Gordon Butcher, of a priceless collection of 34 pieces of Roman gold and silver plate in a field at Thistley Green in Suffolk.

As part of the publicity for the programme, Eton gave an interview to the diarist of the *Evening News* in which he took the opportunity to invite readers who knew any unusual stories of buried treasure to get in touch – especially if the accounts had anything to do with Yugoslavia or Corsica. But just as Ian Fleming found with his *Sunday Times* appeal, Eton was overwhelmed with what he described as 'the usual letters from cranks who wanted me to finance expeditions to raise sunken Spanish galleons or King John's treasure lost in the Wash and so on'.

Among the last of these letters, however, was one which arrived the following March, accompanied by a cutting. It was an article that startled Eton almost as much as when he had read the account of Jakov Jovanovic's death. The piece had been clipped from the *Twickenham & Whitton Chronicle* and was headlined: AMAZING STORY – SEQUEL TO NAZI BLITZ IN YUGOSLAVIA.

The report described the discovery of the gold ingot at Eel Pie Island. But what really grabbed Peter Eton's attention and sent his pulse racing were the details about the *origin* of the bullion:

The *Captain Flint*, a small cabin cruiser recently broken up by Messum's, was found to contain a gold ingot that had been painted black and stowed with bars of pig iron as ballast. The ingot has been identified as one of 800 lost during the war belonging to the Yugoslavian Government. The remainder have never been found.

Eton also read about the boat's peripatetic owner, George Martineau, and how he had left the vessel in Yugoslavia at the outbreak of the war:

> The *Captain Flint* has had an interesting history which began when shortly after the Nazi *Blitzkrieg* on Yugoslavia in 1941, she was stolen and disappeared from the boat yard at Zadar.
>
> In 1946, Major W Follett Routley of the British Consulate in Corsica became inquisitive when he read *Captain Flint* under the paintwork of a boat he had hired for a day's fishing in Bastia. Enquiries revealed that the boat had been sold to the owner by some Italian deserters.

The eagle-eyed consular official had ordered one of his clerks to trace the ownership of the boat and, as he suspected, it had last been registered to a British owner, George Martineau. As the *Twickenham & Whitton Chronicle* added, the late Navy officer's daughter had reclaimed the cruiser, but lack of use had led to it ultimately being broken up for salvage, at which time the ingot was discovered.

After reading the cutting, Peter Eton began to believe he was on the verge of solving one of the great mysteries of the Second World War. And when the diarist of the *Evening News* telephoned him to see if he had received any response to his appeal, he realised he had a better story than he could have possibly imagined – and told the reporter so, although with intriguing reservations. The following day under the heading, DANGEROUS TREASURE, the journalist wrote:

BBC producer Peter Eton is completing one of the strangest dossiers of our time. In it are some of the never published secrets of Rommel's treasure – loot believed to be worth millions of pounds and always before supposed to have been sunk in a boat off the Corsican coast.

Peter Eton has other ideas. For months now he has been following the trail. But he is keeping his findings to himself. Almost every person who has had anything to do with the treasure has mysteriously disappeared.

Eton was certainly guilty of adding a little spice to the account for the benefit of the readers of the *Evening News*. But he was actually far from convinced that the booty from Yugoslavia *was* Rommel's Gold. He certainly had proof that a boat had been used to transport the loot to Corsica. The question now was: where was the rest?

The continuing demands of his job allowed Peter Eton only occasional moments to go on with his investigations into the mystery gold. One week in the summer, he spent a few days in the Twickenham area looking into the story of the *Captain Flint*, but all vestiges of the cabin cruiser had long gone from Messum's yard and no one locally was sure about the fate of the gold ingot.

Still, Eton's urge to get to the truth was such that in September he decided to return to Corsica. Once more he took his tape recorder and was soon busy trawling the cafés of Bastia. Again, too, he met up with his old friend, Antoine Nicolai – and this time was in for yet another shock. For when he showed the Corsican fisherman the cutting about the discovery of the *Captain Flint*, and asked the old man if he knew anything about it, Nicolai burst into laughter.

'Of course, I know about the boat. It was *mine*.'

If the two men had not known each other for years, Peter Eton admitted, he would have dismissed such an extraordinary coincidence as some kind of joke. But, bit by bit, he dragged the facts out of his friend.

During the war, Nicolai had smuggled important members of the Maquis to and from Italy on several occasions. But in order to maintain the impression that he was just an ordinary fisherman, he and his older brother André had continued to go fishing from Bastia almost every day, taking care to avoid the mines that the occupying Italians had laid along the coast.

According to Nicolai, the pair were returning home just as darkness was falling one evening in early May 1941, when they almost literally ran into a small cabin cruiser with four men on board. The boat's engine was silent and the craft was moving solely under the power of its sail. The Nicolai brothers could see at a glance that the vessel was not a patrol boat, although the men's voices were unmistakably Italian. Even in the half-light, it was evident they were filthy and unshaven and wearing dirty army uniforms.

After recovering from the initial shock, the two groups began to make halting conversation. The men on the cruiser were anxious to know where they were. When Antoine told them and asked where they had come from, the reply left him almost speechless. 'They told me they had sailed from Yugoslavia,' he informed Peter Eton. 'I knew they must be Italian deserters. But it didn't seem possible they could have sailed over a thousand miles.'

Antoine Nicolai was even more surprised when the Italians offered to sell him the boat. Now they had reached Corsica, they no longer needed it. André whispered to his brother that even if the boat had only been stolen on the mainland, by the look of it there was every chance of making a quick profit if the price was right. A deal for 7,000 francs was quickly made.

Hardly able to believe their luck, the brothers towed the cabin cruiser into a hiding place they knew on the estuary of the River Golo and then used their own boat to drop the group of dishevelled Italians on the outskirts of Bastia as they asked. The Nicolais never saw them again.

When Antoine Nicolai later started to investigate his purchase more carefully he was left in little doubt that the story he had been told was true. The boat was clearly of British origin: it was marked with a Lloyd's registration number and all the maps in the wheelhouse were in English. He also discovered how it had come to be in Corsica from the crayon marks on the maps that showed a route from the port of Zadar to the coast of Corsica, as well as from the boat's log book. Both of these he later gave to Peter Eton.

It seemed the four men – two brothers, Giuseppe and Achille Papini from Sardinia, a Sicilian, Vittore Marcel, and Gavino Bornea from Foggia in Italy – had all been soldiers in the Italian Second Army based at Zadar. In April 1941, the gang, all with records for petty crime, had killed the owner of a villa on the outskirts of the town while committing a robbery.

Fearful of the repercussions, the men had used some of the proceeds of the robbery to buy the *Captain Flint* from the boatyard owner in whose care she had been left. On 15 April they set sail for Corsica where they intended to contact the Papinis' older brother, Leonetto, who had been posted there with the Italian occupation forces. When the quartet set sail they were quite oblivious to the fact that another group of men had already earmarked the craft for an escape and had actually loaded it the previous day.

The Italians deliberately made landfall only where they were familiar with the locality and knew they could obtain fuel and supplies with the minimum of risk. Their first port of call was Manfredonia on the east coast of Italy near Bornea's home. This was followed by a stop at Syracuse in Sicily where Marcel had grown up. However, when heavy weather off the west coast of Sicily began to slow down their progress, the men made a surprising discovery. As one of the group was investigating the hold, he discovered the reason for their sluggish progress – it was packed to the gunnels with wooden boxes.

Without bothering to look into the chests – which all four imagined to be ballast – the Italians pushed a number of them overboard into the churning Mediterranean as they crossed the Gulf of Avola Noto. Twice more, as the boat made its laborious progress towards Corsica, the deserters heaved boxes overboard. The next time was off the island of Marettimo and the last occasion just hours before they caught sight of the coast of Corsica and ran into the Nicolai brothers.

Another drama awaited Antoine and André when they began working on the boat at an isolated stretch of beach near the little village of Casamozza. The boat was in bad shape after its journey from Zadar and a lot of the planking was damaged. The bottom needed scraping and the entire hull required several coats of paint. The vessel also obviously required a new name to complete the disguise, and the brothers opted for the *Mariana*.

For several days the two men were able to work unobserved, bringing their tools and paint to the beach on André's donkey.

Then tragedy struck in the second week of May. A newspaper account from *Nice-Matin* which Antoine Nicolai kept and gave to Peter Eton along with the ship's log told the story in simple detail:

> The customary calm of the inhabitants living in the area of Casamozza was disturbed yesterday by the sound of about twenty explosions. The explosions were described as sounding like an invasion or the bombs of an aircraft, but there were no signs of aircraft in the skies at that time.
>
> When Italian police reached the isolated area, which has been heavily mined against invasion, they discovered an injured man among the sand dunes. He was treated by an Italian doctor at the airport and has been named as Antoine Nicolai, a fisherman, of Bastia. M Nicolai was later transferred to the civil hospital in Bastia where his condition was described last night as *dangereux*.

This account, as Peter Eton discovered, told only half the story. Antoine had already been at work for some time removing from the *Mariana* a number of boxes he had found in the hold, which he described as 'heavy as hell'. He had removed about half a dozen and put them on the dunes when he noticed his brother coming towards him with his donkey.

A moment later and the beach was rocked by explosion after explosion. Even as the effect of the blasts flung him to the ground, Antoine realised what had happened. The donkey must have stepped on a mine and triggered off a linked series of explosions.

As soon as he had recovered sufficiently, Antoine stumbled to where he had last seen his brother. A series of gaping holes

159

dotted the dunes. There was no sign of either André or the donkey. Both had literally been blown apart.

Antoine reported André's death to the Italian authorities, who apparently took pity on him and did not enquire too deeply why the pair had been in a prohibited zone. He, of course, made no mention of the boat they had been working on.

It was a sadder and wiser man who went gingerly back on to the beach at Casamozza some weeks later to complete the renovation of the former *Captain Flint* and then sail her to Bastia harbour. He never gave another thought to the boxes he had been dumping on the beach before the explosion, which were now scattered to the winds.

For the remainder of the war and after peace returned to the island in 1943, Antoine Nicolai worked 'his' boat in and out of Bastia. Then came the day three years later when her real identity was spotted by the British Consul, Major Routley, and the *Mariana* was confiscated.

With a shrug of his shoulders, the Corsican told Peter Eton that he had parted company with the cruiser as casually as she had come into his possession. The boat had more than earned the price he had paid and it seemed only right to him that the *Captain Flint* should go back to the daughter of the brave Englishman who had lost his life in the war.

After Eton had listened to his friend's story, he stayed on Corsica for a few more days tying up the loose ends of the mystery. It was clear that the Germans who had stolen the gold bullion after ambushing the Yugoslavian truck had taken the boxes to Zadar and there planned to flee the country in any suitable boat they could find in the harbour. The soldiers' choice had fallen on the *Captain Flint*. But things had gone very wrong for them when the Italian deserters had spirited away the cruiser – its golden cargo and all – from right under their noses.

If local gossip was correct, the bewildered and angry Germans had no alternative but to return to their Recce Battalion, claiming they had lost their way in the mountains and ended up at Zadar. All four were believed to have been posted to Libya in April 1942 to serve in the 21st Panzer Division of the Afrika Korps. Only one was thought to have survived.

The one thing that Peter Eton was now more convinced of than ever was that this bullion had nothing to do with the legend of Rommel's Gold. The ingots from Yugoslavia that the Italian deserters had thrown into the sea – save the one found in England – had never been intended for Hitler. They were the booty of war that a group of greedy and unscrupulous Germans and Italians had succeeded only in consigning to the depths of the Mediterranean.

Eton returned to England and continued his career with the BBC. But still the urge to look for the remaining gold ingots intruded into his thoughts every now and then. A year later, he finally decided the time had come to take unpaid leave from the BBC and carry out a proper search. He would take a mine detector and perhaps hire a boat with divers and lifting equipment if the bullion was found on the seabed.

So buoyed up was Eton by the challenge that he gave a revealing interview to his local paper in Lewes, the *Sussex Express and County Herald*, just before Christmas 1949. The story was headlined HE'S ON THE TRACK OF A MILLION POUNDS and must surely have caught the attention of anyone in austerity-bound England who dreamed of finding a fortune:

Off to Corsica early next year is Peter Eton, the well-known BBC producer. He'll not search for material for a new radio programme. He's after a million pounds in gold bars. That's his estimate of the value of Rommel's treasure which he believes is lying under the desolate sand dunes of Bastia, Corsica. As far as Eton – and other people – are concerned, Rommel's treasure exists and only wants finding.

The only thing false about it, they believe, is the name given to this treasure. It has nothing to do with Rommel – only that the men who collected the gold eventually served under his command.

Eton told the newspaper's reporter the facts about the Germans' seizure of the gold bullion in Yugoslavia and their dash to the port of Zadar:

Eventually the gold was placed on a boat, but fate stepped in to stop the looters enjoying the benefits of their ill-gotten gains. Some Italian deserters, with no knowledge of the vast sum on board, took the boat and escaped. They sailed her to Corsica and beached the craft near Bastia.

There the Italians sold the boat to some local Corsicans. No one in the transaction knew treasure was involved. The 'buyers' of this treasure ship started to unload her and stacked the gold, that would be 'disguised', of course, maybe as pig-iron. Unfortunately, a donkey being used by the men stepped on a booby trap which immediately set off a train of landmines. The gold was blown into the air and scattered over the sand dunes.

Peter Eton concluded:

> Today with shifting sands and rough seas, the ingots are
> probably buried to a depth of 10 feet. Last month I went to
> Corsica and talked to a local inhabitant who is pretty
> certain of the area in which the gold is lying. It'll be a tricky
> business – there are still landmines there – but I'm
> determined to have a go.

And have a go Eton certainly did. He returned to Corsica
with two friends and scoured the dunes around Casamozza
between the placid waters of the Etang de Biguglia and the
estuary of the River Golo. He did not find as much as a
fragment of gold.

Peter Eton's obsession with that bullion incorrectly labelled
Rommel's Gold continued to haunt him until his death in 1963.
He produced several more progammes for BBC Radio,
including the successful series *Just William* and the less well
known *Meet the Huggets*, which ran from 1953 to 1961. Later he
left the BBC and went to work for Granada TV in Manchester.

He was also the producer of the legendary *Goon Show*
starring Spike Milligan, Harry Secombe and Peter Sellers from
the winter of 1952 to the end of 1956. In what may have been
almost a deliberate attempt to exorcise his obsession, Eton gave
the manic trio access to the information he had so painstakingly
gathered for a show entitled *Rommel's Treasure* which was
broadcast on 25 October 1955 (it was originally announced as
The Search for Rommel's Treasure).

Although it was certainly far from the best episode in that
wonderful series, the story played fast and loose with the legend

in a tale of the trio searching for a treasure that is buried three feet *above* ground! The programme is, though, still fondly remembered by enthusiasts of the show.

Perhaps the most extraordinary feature of the looted Yugoslavian gold bullion is that the remnants should have ended up by pure chance on the same stretch of coast where Peter Fleig and the German Army officers had deliberately dropped the real Rommel's Gold. It is an amazing coincidence and has contributed to the confusion and misinformation that surrounds the whole mystery. However, if no one since Peter Eton's modest efforts has tried to locate the ingots – which in all probability still lie somewhere beneath the shifting sands at Casamozza – quite the reverse is the case with the treasure trove from Tunisia hidden in the bay.

Indeed, in the intervening years, a number of very determined hunters have explored the waters around Bastia. They have come with ever-improving underwater technology and scientific expertise, all driven by the same obsession to solve the mystery...

9

Search of The Dreamweaver

There is convincing evidence that the Frenchman, Louis Bordes, who saw Peter Fleig and the four German officers hiding the six cases of Rommel's Gold off the east coast of Corsica, was probably the first person to go searching for the treasure after the failure of the French expedition in the summer of 1948. Why he did not try earlier can now only be a matter for conjecture.

According to a story in *L'Espoir de Nice*, Bordes returned to Corsica after reading reports of Loebenberg's expedition and recruited the help of a boat owner in Poreta. The Frenchman had in the interim taught himself to be a skilful diver and soon became a familiar figure to local people as he set off, day after day, to explore the seabed near Cap Sud. Despite their wry smiles, the locals knew all about the legend and none of them were quite prepared to write Bordes off as a madman. Obsessed, certainly. 'He had become infected by the fever to find Rommel's Gold,' the newspaper added, 'but despite all his dives, M Bordes had no success.'

It was, in fact, to be almost a decade after the Loebenberg search that another major attempt to locate the treasure took place, although Peter Eton, for one, was told in 1956 that 'plenty of people have been looking for it ever since 1948.'

Typical of these was another Frenchman, Henry Helle, who was bitten by the bug in 1951 and spent two months on his boat, the *Starlena*, off the Etang de Biguglia. He even briefly employed a professional Italian diver named Kantrellieri to help in the exploration, but was forced to give up empty-handed when the weather turned bad in late summer.

The following year, however, Helle was invited to join a new and much better equipped expedition financed by a wealthy American treasure hunter from New York named Ruth Bond. Mrs Bond had become increasingly fascinated by the stories of the legendary Rommel's Gold she had read in the American press. She had the money to finance a proper maritime search for it, but not the expertise, so she decided to call in a retired British seaman who she knew had plenty of experience. He was Lieutenant-Commander Stewart Pears, a former Royal Navy stalwart who had served in both world wars and was an expert on Mediterranean waters.

Pears had risen through the ranks and seen action on HMS *Falmouth* and *Oak* during 1914–18. In the 1930s he had been transferred to research and experimental duties in Plymouth and also spent several years in the Mediterranean. During the Second World War, he had been Superintendent of the Navy's Experimental Establishment at Pendine and completed his career on the Ordnance Board before retiring in 1956. An energetic man with a passion for sailing, Pears listed his hobbies in *Who's Who* as 'anything out of doors'.

In the spring of 1957 he accepted Mrs Bond's invitation to join the treasure hunt off Corsica and took charge of a 45-ton yacht, *Romany Maid*, which had been equipped with the latest underwater exploration equipment as well as heavy-duty cranes and winching gear. Also on board was Henry Helle, ready to make information from his previous year's work available to the search team.

The exploration that Pears supervised that summer around the bay of Bastia was painstaking and methodical, his team of divers working in pairs as they covered designated areas of the ocean floor. But once again the search was rewarded only with failure. 'We concentrated on an area off Cape Bianca which seemed to coincide with the most precise information we could obtain,' the Lieutenant-Commander told reporters in a rare press conference reported by the *Evening News* of London. 'But I am afraid we have found no trace of treasure at all. Not a thing.'

Ruth Bond was not yet quite ready to give up and financed a second expedition the following year. Over fifteen years had now passed since the six cases had been sent to the bottom of the sea and there were those who believed that sand and silt had probably obliterated all trace of them.

Although the American millionairess had no more luck than in the previous year, in 1960 it did seem as if the sceptics might be proved wrong when another French diver caused a stir in the media by claiming that he had actually seen some mysterious objects on the seabed – albeit some miles to the south. The man's name was Jean-Napoléon Peretti and he talked with some excitement to journalists in the August of that year.

'I was doing some underwater exploring at a depth of about 15 metres along the craggy coast of Porto Vecchio when I saw something in a hollow on the seabed, ' he was quoted in *Paris-Press*. 'They looked like waterproof lead containers protected by a steel net covered in mud. I tried to move one of the cases, but it was far too heavy. The effort of trying to pull off the netting exhausted me and I had to swim back to the shore.'

Peretti claimed that there might have been as many as thirty crates in the hollow and agreed that it was some distance from the area generally associated with the missing treasure. He added that he had made several more dives, but had been unable to find the spot again.

If this report only added to the frustration of those hoping to get closer to the treasure, it certainly kept alive the interest of others who had followed news of the hunt over the years. Among their number was an American marine expert who had been pushing back the boundaries of deep-sea exploration for years and – almost twenty years to the day after the saga of Rommel's Gold had begun – would bring the most scientifically advanced ship and equipment to Corsica for yet another attempt to find the missing millions. His name was Edwin Link and he had a well-earned reputation for beating the odds where few other people were even prepared to take the price.

Edwin Albert Link was born in 1904 in the small midwestern state of Indiana, home to a number of famous American pioneers including Daniel Boone and Abraham Lincoln. At the age of six, Ed was moved east with his family and older brother, George, to Binghamton in New York state when his father was appointed manager of the Automatic Music Company, manufacturers of pipe organs.

From an early age, young Ed loved gadgets – spending hours taking mechanical things apart to find out how they worked –

although at school he proved to be something of a rebel, stubborn and persistent in the face of authority, and a bit of a dreamer. Although raised far from the sea, he admitted later to often losing himself in thoughts about the depths of the ocean. At the age of twelve this dreaming took more solid form when he designed his own submarine.

Ed's craft had space for a crew of ten, and was fitted with a retractable gun and its own supply of torpedoes. The young inventor described the vessel's method of propulsion in these words: 'This Sub can go eaqually [sic] as good under water as on the surface. It runs with a gasoline engine all the time. The Link consumer [engine] enables it to do so.'

If ever the future of a young man was encapsulated in a single event during his childhood, then this invention by Ed Link probably fits that criterion perfectly – although the inventor was to admit many years later in the *Smithsonian Magazine*: 'Unfortunately, it wasn't very practical – it most assuredly would have sunk.' Small wonder that Link was to be labelled 'The Dreamweaver' by a close friend, Joe MacInnis. Unlike most dreamers, however, he would prove to be a man who got things done.

In 1918, after the traumatic divorce of his parents, Ed went to live with his mother who supported her two sons as a travelling singer. This unsettled life did little to encourage the younger boy to study – until the day he discovered mechanics at the Los Angeles Polytechnic High School. The courses in mechanical drawing, machine shop and foundry work fired his imagination and he began to develop the skill at problem-solving and dexterity with tools that would provide the basics for his future. He also caught the bug for flying.

Ed was forced to supplement the family's meagre income by working in a service garage during his spare time so there was little cash for flying lessons. Nevertheless, he scraped together $50 and made his first flight from Chaplin's Field on Wilshire Boulevard. The hair-raising ride in a rackety Curtiss Jenny biplane was something he never forgot – and made him all the more determined to earn his wings.

At the age of eighteen, Ed dropped out of school and returned with his mother and brother to Binghamton, where he was given a job at his father's old company repairing and rebuilding pianos and organs. This work often required him to travel around the country and he seized every opportunity to take more flying lessons from the barnstorming pilots who were then enjoying nationwide popularity with their daring aerial displays. He kept abreast of the latest developments in mechanics by avidly reading *Popular Science* and *Popular Mechanics*.

His thirst for knowledge also made him aware of the dangers of flying. In the late 1920s, statistics showed that the flying lessons on offer were inadequate at best and the number of deaths in both private and commercial aviation was mounting every year. It was clear that far too many pilots were flying by the seat of their pants. Ed Link then had the first of the brainwaves that were to make his name: why not learn to fly *on the ground*.

Link was convinced that if he could develop a machine that simulated real flight, new pilots would be able to take to the air better prepared. So in 1928 he began to construct a miniature aeroplane with wings, fuselage and a cockpit complete with stick, rudder bar and compass. He called it 'the first primary flight trainer' but soon his contraption – which could turn, bank and revolve as well as pitch and roll exactly like the real thing – would become known everywhere as the Link Trainer.

In the interim, Ed succeeded in gaining his own pilot's licence and bought a plane of his own, one of the earliest Cessna Model AAs. In the years of the Depression that followed, he was able to supplement his earnings at the Automatic Music Company by giving ground lessons in the trainer as well as instruction flights and pleasure rides in the Cessna. He also had the idea of 'aerial advertising', flying his plane across the night sky trailing illuminated signs that advertised his sponsors' products, such as Spauldings Bread, Enna Jettick Shoes and Utica Club Beer.

However, the best thing to come out of this period of his life as far as Ed was concerned was a chance meeting with a pretty young journalist, Marion Clayton, newly recruited to the staff of the *Binghamton Press*. Their shared love of aviation and thirst for adventure led to marriage in 1931 and Marion was to prove the ideal organiser of Ed's expeditions and the chronicler of his restless search for new frontiers to conquer.

The advent of the Second World War saw the Link Trainer come into its own as the US Air Force scrambled to train more pilots for the conflict against the Axis powers. Subsequently, it was estimated that the trainers were used to instruct more than half a million airmen throughout the world.

The war also gave Ed Link an opportunity to combine two of his greatest interests – aviation and the sea. At the time, a workable aircraft carrier was then only a concept, but Link went a step further and visualised the day when fleets of seaplanes would operate against the enemy from bases on the ocean. In

171

preparation, he created a new version of the Link Trainer with the lower half of its fuselage sunk in a tank of water. Rookie pilots then sat at the controls of the 'Aqua Trainer' while it rose from the water in a simulated take-off.

Because of the Allies' huge demand for the Link Trainer throughout the war, at its end Ed Link was a wealthy man – a millionaire in fact. Soon, though, the demands of running the business began to pall on him, especially when the tang of ozone hit his nostrils. He decided it was time he and Marion left America to pursue another dream – probing the hidden depths of the sea.

It would not be long, in fact, before he would find a more specific and enduring obsession – searching for treasure lost at sea. An obsession that would ultimately lead him to search for Rommel's Gold.

Later in his life, Ed Link was never slow to admit that he was not sure what he was looking for when he and Marion set off on their journeys in the streamlined wooden yawl, the *Blue Heron*, which they purchased in 1948. At first it was merely a question of learning the techniques of sailing, and the art of navigation and being constantly alert to the power of the sea. Then the pair started making longer trips around the Atlantic coast to Canada, Florida and the Caribbean. They even took part in ocean racing with typical enthusiasm, determination and success.

But in the spring of 1951, a profound change occurred in Ed's life, as Marion herself has described in her book, *Sea Diver* (1958):

He was a little bored with ocean racing, now that he had conquered it. Before I could believe it, I found myself embarked on a new adventure. We were members of an expedition which had gathered to dive on the wrecks of three ancient sailing ships on the reefs off the Florida Keys. I should have realised right then and there that one of those crucial times had arrived in Ed's life when it was essential for him to progress on to a new enthusiasm...

The moment of change could not have been more dramatic. While the couple were in the Florida Keys, they were told that what looked like an old shipwreck had been spotted just off the coast. Ed, who just happened to have some diving equipment on board the *Blue Heron*, went overboard without a moment's hesitation. When he returned to the surface some twenty minutes later he announced breathlessly to his wife that he had found treasure: a Spanish cannon dated 1617.

Journalist Arthur Herzog, who wrote a number of articles about Ed Link, has vividly described this defining moment in his subject's life in 'Explorer of the Underwater Frontier', published in *True* magazine, December 1964:

Overnight the Links became treasure hunters, scudding about the Caribbean and bringing up pieces-of-eight, ballast and other cannons – finds they would probably think fairly commonplace today. In smart skin-diving circles an old cannon, unless it happens to be an English bronze or a rare Spanish gun coated with platinum and worth its weight in income tax, is not a very sophisticated find. *Link, however, was just getting started* [My italics].

173

Herzog could not have been more astute in his judgement. The discovery filled Link's head with dreams of buried treasure, as well as setting him entirely new challenges in underwater mechanics. In the past it had often been the depth at which such hoards lay that had defeated searchers. If he was to succeed where they had failed, Ed knew, he would have to develop completely new submersible equipment.

After Ed's modest triumph in finding the Spanish cannon, he did not need asking twice to take part in an expedition that had been set up to explore three wrecks lying off the coast of Marathon in the Florida Keys. The decision enabled him to meet several veteran treasure hunters whose knowledge and advice would be of great value to him – in particular Art McKee, a well-known professional diver and owner of the Museum of Sunken Treasure on Plantation Key, and Bill Thompson from Marathon, who had actually discovered the trio of wrecks.

Ed Link's first contribution to the underwater hunt was a revolutionary apparatus developed from the original aqualung that had first been tested in France in 1943 by the veteran diver Frederic Dumas. Ed's new aqualung consisted of a face mask and separate mouthpiece, with a regulator and air hose attached to a tank of compressed air strapped to the diver's back. It proved more versatile and allowed for longer periods of searching than the earlier 'hookah gear', which had consisted of a full-face mask and air hose joined to a compressor on an accompanying ship. There was no holding Ed back from diving with the other more experienced divers and the success of the treasure hunt had a striking effect on both him and his wife, as Marion was to write later:

174

By the time the expedition was over Ed and I were confirmed treasure seekers. We had been afflicted with a contagion which was to lead us on strange and unexpected adventures. Following its onset we found ourselves unable to resist tales of treasure-laden ships lying upon the ocean floor, their contents still untouched. We felt sure that they only awaited our coming to surrender vast quantities of riches.

The first haul off Marathon gave every sign that this might be true. The divers' finds included a hoard of coins dated as late as 1720 and a 2,000-pound cannon, evidently from a British ship. Subsequent research in Washington established that the vessel was the HMS *Looe* which had been patrolling the seas between Cuba and the Florida Keys when it was reported lost in a storm. Another of the wrecks was thought to be that of a Spanish vessel, the *Snow*, which had been captured by the *Looe* and was under tow when disaster struck.

For Ed Link, The Dreamweaver, the development of the aqualung opened up whole new possibilities for undersea exploration. Apart from treasure hunting, he pondered on whether the freedom of movement the apparatus permitted would allow him to explore some of history's great submerged mysteries. There is evidence from his notes that Link put on his list the idea of looking for evidence of the lost continent of Atlantis, tracing the route and landfall of Christopher Columbus in the New World, and looking for the last resting place of the great discoverer's ill-fated flagship, the *Santa Maria*, arguably the most famous shipwreck in history.

Realising that it was now becoming increasingly difficult to carry all the equipment needed to hunt for undersea 'gold' on the *Blue Heron* – whether his quarry was lost treasure or marine archaeology – Link knew he needed a bigger boat: one that had a crane, winches and plenty of storage space. In May 1952, he purchased *Sea Diver*, a 65-foot trawler-like yacht with an eight-cylinder Caterpillar diesel engine capable of generating 300hp.

The first voyage of the *Sea Diver* ended in disaster when the vessel struck the seabed in Key Largo and had to limp back to Miami for major repairs. Ed, though, made full use of this lull in his adventures to design and test more ingenious undersea equipment. During his enforced stay on land he created a small, glass-bottomed boat for observation just beneath the surface of the water, a magnetometer – a piece of specialised equipment that picks up kinks in the earth's magnetic field caused by extraneous metal – for underwater detection when visible evidence of ancient wrecks was virtually nonexistent, and an 'airlift' that used suction to bring up small artefacts from the depths.

Throughout 1953, Ed and the *Sea Diver* roamed further afield; news of the discovery of cannons and coins in the Florida Keys had created a kind of 'California Gold Rush' in the area, which became a target for all manner of amateur treasure hunters. However, interest in Link's work earned serious attention from *National Geographic* and *Life* magazines, and Ed co-operated on several feature articles that helped to open up the wonders of the undersea world and reveal the treasures he had found.

In 1955, Link began his most ambitious treasure hunt to date when he set out to locate the remains of the Spanish galleon, *Neustra Senora de la Concepcion*, which had sailed from Havana for Spain in September 1659, carrying gold, silver and precious jewels said to be worth millions. The vessel had foundered in a storm near the aptly named Silver Shoals, some 80 miles from the Dominican Republic. The location had a reputation – evidently well-earned – of being one of the most dangerous areas of reefs in that part of the world. It was seen as a Mecca for treasure hunters, too, because of the fabulous wealth on board the Spanish ship – but only a handful of the most reckless had ever tried to locate the wreck.

As the *Sea Diver* traversed the area of forty square miles, Link made use of an ancient map prepared by an American sea captain, William Phipps. In 1687 Phipps had himself searched for the treasure, consisting of valuables whose estimated worth even then was £300,000. Link now had the very latest technology at his disposal in the shape of a new invention: a glass-bottomed, shallow-draft cruiser powered by a water jet that could explore areas of the shoals inaccessible to any normal vessel. He had named the craft *Reef Diver*.

The search proved long and arduous and not without its dangers; Link was doubly careful as he had no desire to suffer the same fate as the Spanish seamen three centuries earlier. However, fortune favoured his desire to locate the position where the *Neustra Senora* lay, although the heavy waves continually breaking over the reefs allowed only a handful of dives to take place. But using the magnetometer and some controlled blasting with dynamite, Link and his team were able to recover an anchor, part of a gun barrel and the oxidised remains of a hoard of silver coins.

With the seasonal storms rapidly approaching, they finally had to leave the wreck of the great ship in its watery grave. But Ed Link carried away vivid memories of the site and the giant formations of coral, which he described as 'rugged and weird and like a trip to the moon'.

177

The following year, 1956, The Dreamweaver raised his sights once again and set out for Jamaica. What had taken his interest now was the legendary archaeological mystery of the sunken city of Port Royal off Kingston Harbour.

Rumours abounded about the once famous and wealthy British colony that had disappeared beneath the waves as the result of a violent earthquake in 1692 that killed over 2,000 people. A number of houses were said to be still intact in the gloomy depths and there was even supposed to be a great cathedral standing, its roof held up by huge columns. All over the site, tradition had it, hoards of gold bars, silverware and precious artefacts valued at hundreds of thousands of pounds lay awaiting reclamation.

Consulting local archives and utilising the equipment on *Sea Diver* – in particular a portable fathometer – Ed Link came to the conclusion that the rubble of the lost city now lay about sixty feet deep in the murky waters. There was, though, no sign of any standing houses or the fabled cathedral.

The odds on there being buried treasure were very much better. Prior to the earthquake Port Royal had been a major trading point, renowned equally for its wealth and debauchery. Among the most frequent visitors had been the buccaneers who brought loot from the New World to sell on to local merchants.

It seemed very probable that a quantity of this gold, silver and jewellery would have been in port before leaving for Europe and had been lost in the earthquake with everything else. A fact, substantiated by a local clergyman, Reverend John Divine, who survived the disaster and wrote home to his relatives in England that 'the coin and bullion lost is not to be computed, but many people think at least to the value of 400,000 pounds.'

Armed with this information, Ed Link started to dive in the vicinity where he believed the warehouses for the pirates' booty might have been situated. He was immediately faced with the problem of jagged coral reefs, combined with visibility underwater that extended for only a few feet. There were also sharks and barracudas to beware.

The contrast with the clear waters to which Ed Link and his team were used to could not have been more stark, but the thrill of the hunt drove them all on. Among the first discoveries was ample evidence of Port Royal's debauchery – thousands of bottles, the oldest of which were onion-shaped and encrusted with the coral of centuries. The airlift also brought up to the decks of the *Sea Diver* a number of artefacts made of copper, pottery and stone that clearly dated from the period of the earthquake.

By his own admission, Ed dreamed for weeks that the divers might find one of the great iron-bound chests in which the wealthy men of Port Royal kept their gold, silver, jewellery and coins – banks, of course, being unknown. The discovery of pieces of wood in a section of brick wall briefly ignited this dream, but all that came to the surface were everyday items of decorated porcelain, musket flints, clay pipes and tokens... along with even more bottles.

A large cannon marked with the royal symbol of a Crown and Rose was to prove the only other major discovery of the expedition. However, Ed and his team had done much to demonstrate the value of his underwater equipment as well as making the first important survey of sunken Port Royal.

Ed Link had also reached another important conclusion. If he was going to extend his treasure hunting further in localities such as this one – or deeper in the oceans of the world – he needed a still bigger boat.

Instead of buying an existing vessel, however, Link set about designing his own purpose-built craft. The result was a 93-foot, steel, double-hulled yacht with two GM6-110 diesel engines generating 240hp and capable of cruising at ten knots. Costing a total of $500,000, *Sea Diver II* was launched in April 1959 and was undeniably the most perfectly suited boat for underwater archaeology of its time.

Along with a unique viewing chamber from which to survey the deeps, Ed added the rest of the technology he had so painstakingly devised and tested in recent years including the *Reef Diver*, two high-pressure 2,500lb air compressors, a six-ton lift and a submersible decompression chamber (SDC) for divers engaged on deep-water exploration. It would require nothing less, as Ed Link was to discover, to seek out something as elusive as Rommel's Gold.

In 1960 The Dreamweaver extended his horizons further still and made his first trip in *Sea Diver II* to the Mediterranean. Here he cruised around the Holy Land before setting course for the Greek islands – but, unfortunately, he soon found that the local laws prevented him from carrying out the kind of free-ranging explorations he so enjoyed.

Greece, in particular, with its long tradition of buried treasure, proved an absolute nightmare for Link. The authorities completely misunderstood his intent; almost from the moment that *Sea Diver II* arrived off the coast of Rhodes he and his crew were marked down as bounty hunters looking to plunder valuable deep–sea artefacts. As Link himself wrote later: 'We were full of high ideals and delusions of maybe finding something comparable to the Venus de Milo which we could contribute to their museums for posterity. But no sooner had we dropped anchor than we were introduced to Greek red tape and rubber stamps and even found ourselves being followed at one time from island to island by a gunboat!'

No matter where the vessel went as she sailed innocently through the Greek islands, Ed Link found it impossible to get permission to dive, despite all the assurances he gave the police and customs officials. For their part, the crew were constantly aware of eyes watching them, in particular a man in a small rowing boat posing as a fisherman who was never far away. Finally, on 4 August, Ed Link was arrested and charged with diving at Perchora in the Bay of Corinth 'without the necessary authority and with intent to illegally export artefacts'. He was taken ashore and the boat impounded.

Thanks to the intervention of lawyers from the American Embassy and the failure of the prosecution to bring any evidence of illegal activity, Link was cleared of the charge, although not until after a lengthy wrangle and even the threat of imprisonment. But the episode left him bitter and determined never to return to Greek waters again: 'It was really a sort of farce – we never should have been charged in the first place,' he said.

Sea Diver II was freed by the Greek authorities on 16 September and Ed and his crew sailed immediately from Athens feeling 'mighty relieved'. As the craft passed the beautiful Peloponnese islands before heading back to America, Ed was probably in no mood to recall the action that had occurred there in 1944 at Navarino Bay when the first Allied troops had landed in Greece and begun driving out the German occupiers.

It might just have been an omen, however, for within six months he was back in the Mediterranean. This time the objective would be a wartime treasure trove that had attracted the reputation of being the most valuable modern underwater hoard still unclaimed. Rommel's Gold was an irresistible challenge to a man like Ed Link.

Two men were responsible for Link's interest in the treasure: a larger-than-life Irish nobleman, Lord John Kilbracken, and a Belgian, Robert Stenuit, arguably the finest deep-sea diver of his generation. The trio had been brought together by chance, but became united in an extraordinary and secretive attempt to raise the lost booty in 1963.

John Godley, Lord Kilbracken, was the latest in the line of a merchant family who had moved to Ireland in the seventeenth century and been ennobled in 1909. Born at the family seat, Killegar, County Leitrim, in 1920, Kilbracken grew up with a love of adventure and his reckless exploits as a Swordfish pilot in the Fleet Air Arm during 1940–45 formed the basis of his best-selling autobiography, *Bring Back My Stringbag* (1948). After the war, Kilbracken took his seat as a backbencher in the House of Lords and earned his living as an author and journalist. A man of diverse interests, he wrote the definitive biography of the notorious art forger, Van Meegeren, as well as the prize-winning series of 'Easy Way' books intended to help readers identify species of birds, trees and wild flowers.

He loved travel, too, and in the 1960s began contributing articles to the prestigious *National Geographic* magazine. It was a commission to write about undersea exploration that led him to meet Ed Link in 1962. The forthright and determined

American and the gregarious, bearded Irishman took an immediate liking to one another.

They first met in London, when Link told Kilbracken all about his 'Man-In-Sea' project to make the seas more accessible. What the American proposed was a new submersible decompression chamber – a 'pressurised underwater house' – that could be lowered to the ocean bed and there used as the base for one or more divers to carry out exploration and experimentation.

After his years of undersea exploration, Link appreciated the problems of working deep in the ocean – nitrogen narcosis (the effect of nitrogen on the blood that can cause a euphoric diver to remove his mask and drown), oxygen poisoning, and the bends, caused by staying down too long and coming up too fast. He hoped that in his SDC, divers would be able to live and work down below for weeks on end, requiring decompression only when the chamber returned to the surface.

On 8 August 1962, the Irishman joined Link on *Sea Diver II* to watch the first experiments with 'the world's first manned lockout submersible'. In a subsequent article for *National Geographic*, 'The Long, Deep Dive' (May 1963), he described the SDC as resembling a large aluminium cylinder with small, fish-eye portholes that jutted out at an angle on each side. There was a lockout hatch at one end of the machine.

Being a firm believer in the old adage that he would never ask anyone to do something he would not do himself, Ed himself had already carried out a number of tests with the SDC and on 28 August made the world's first sustained helium–oxygen dive near Villefranche-sur-Mer on the French Riviera. The dive went to a depth of 60 feet, Link remaining below surface for eight hours.

The Dreamweaver emerged exhausted but triumphant from his SDC, announcing that it was now ready for a full test. This was to be carried out by another friend, the Belgian Robert Stenuit, who was on his way to join the *Sea Diver*.

Stenuit was a remarkable man who had been planning a career as a lawyer until he read a book on undersea adventure and overnight changed his mind. Like Ed Link, he had become fascinated with underwater archaeology and the search for buried treasure. He had devoted thousands of hours to exploring the oceans of the world before taking part in the SDC's attempt at a record dive.

After a preliminary dive on 4 September, Robert Stenuit waited for ideal weather conditions. Three days later he went for the 'big one': diving to 200 feet and remaining there for 26 hours, he thus established the record for the world's longest, deepest dive. Stenuit said he would have stayed longer, but when the helium supply suddenly reduced, it was decided to bring the SDC back to the surface.

Lord Kilbracken had watched the events from the deck of the *Sea Diver*. He had grown to like and admire Stenuit and was convinced that the Belgian's achievement would help to revolutionise oil and offshore diving in dangerous areas such as the North Sea. As a journalist, he had a scoop on his hands. Robert Stenuit himself commented on the historic dive in an article for *National Geographic* in April 1965: 'To live, eat, sleep and work in depths so far unreachable by free divers was the most extraordinary adventure of which a diver might dream. The 200 foot dive proved that Ed Link's colossal tin can and its occupant could function as planned.'

During the elated celebrations on board *Sea Diver*, Link,

Stenuit and Kilbracken spent hours swapping stories of treasure hunting. All three were familiar with the wrecks that lay scattered across the Mediterranean, but the story that most excited their imaginations on that trip – as Stenuit was to reveal later in his book, *Ces Mondes secrets où j'ai plongé* – was that of Rommel's Gold.

All three men returned to their respective homes that winter. But they came together again in the Mediterranean in the spring of 1963 when Ed Link recommenced his experiments with the SDC. His diary for the month of April – now deposited in the archives of Binghamton University – is, for once, curiously lacking in detail and more than a little mysterious: 'I had just completed docking Sea Diver at her berth in Monaco harbour *after a two week trip to the waters off eastern Corsica where we had been testing a new type of proton magnetometer for search purposes* [my italics] when I was told Admiral Edward Stephen had been trying to reach me from Washington.'

Although Link explained the importance of Admiral Stephen's telephone call, only Robert Stenuit has gone on record about the two-week 'trip' off the coast of Corsica. According to him, the *Sea Diver* was looking for Rommel's Gold.

It appeared that during the winter of 1962, Kilbracken had been able to track down the one man said to know the whereabouts of the Nazi plunder – Peter Fleig. We have this on the evidence of Charles Van Deusen, who was still looking for clues about the missing gold and wrote a footnote to this effect in another article for the December issue of *True* magazine: 'As this is going to press, an Irish adventurer, Lord Kilbracken, has announced that he has found Peter Fleig, alive and still talkative – but he won't tell where.'

This story was read by Ed Link who put a copy in his own files at Binghamton. Intriguingly, there is a notation on it in Ed's handwriting to 'Send to Kilbracken.'

According to Robert Stenuit, there were six men on board the *Sea Diver* off Corsica that April: Kilbracken, Fleig, Link, Stenuit and two others, a man named Faller and a lawyer representing Peter Fleig. The Belgian diver provided no name for the lawyer and claimed that Faller was present because he 'had a map of the treasure'. Like Van Deusen, Stenuit credits Kilbracken with finding Fleig after his disappearance from Corsica. Stenuit adds a further element of mystery to the gathering: 'Before embarking, the crew had promised to reveal nothing for ten years concerning the area of their search and the results of the expedition. A contract stipulated each one's share if the search was successful.'

There are no precise details of the subsequent search on record. Ed Link's admission that he was testing a magnetometer indicates that such a device was likely to have been employed. Although limited in its range and difficult to use in certain sea conditions, the gadget, which is towed by a ship in parallel runs of five yards apart, would have been able to locate six metal cases if it passed close enough to reveal their presence by the needle on the machine's recording screen.

The *Sea Diver*'s log indicates that the SDC was also used during this period. The depth at which Rommel's Gold had been buried was certainly within its capabilities and Stenuit confirms that he did dive on several occasions. 'We had several false starts,' he wrote. 'I dived in the same sandy area on the sea bottom. We carried on our search day after day, tirelessly, but ultimately in vain.'

It is not difficult to visualise the experienced Belgian slipping down into the deeps in the SDC capsule surrounded by depth gauges, carbon dioxide indicators, emergency breathing apparatus and instruments for measuring the proportions of oxygen and helium. Or to imagine the pressure on his eardrums and lungs increasing as the mixture of oxy-helium inside the machine grew ever more dense.

Stenuit would have felt the chains lowering him through the deep indigo of the sea and peered through the lookout window at the front of the machine waiting for the gentle bump as it struck the ocean bed. Once in position, he would have been confident that if he found the chests they could be hauled into the SDC and raised to the surface with greater ease than any ordinary crane or winch could offer.

Yet Rommel's Gold was to elude this group of searchers just as it had done those before them. Not due to a lack of determination or expertise, however, but because of a totally unexpected disaster that Ed Link heard about when he spoke to Admiral Stephen, the man who had been trying to contact him in his absence.

From the American commander he learned that on 10 April the nuclear powered submarine USS *Thresher* had sunk somewhere in the North Atlantic with the loss of all 129 members of its crew. It was the worst submarine disaster in US Navy history and Link was asked if he would join the Deep Submergence Systems Review Group (DSSRG) to investigate the tragedy.

Patriotism had always come a long way ahead of personal ambition where Ed Link was concerned – and certainly ahead of any hunt for buried treasure. He agreed to travel to Washington immediately. It was left to Robert Stenuit to write finis to the search off Corsica: 'Yes, we failed – but we did learn this. There *is* maybe something metallic in the very spot that Peter Fleig told us. A something that according to him is six iron boxes containing ten million British pounds sterling in gold and diamonds.'

The Belgian diver's account gives no further information about the location that he searched so painstakingly. However, he does admit to getting a rather uncomfortable feeling during the exploration that remained with him long afterwards. Stenuit became convinced that there were others looking for the gold. People he felt there were good reasons for not naming. A group of criminals, in fact, whose very name inspired fear throughout the entire Mediterranean.

The Mafia.

10

The Criminal Conspiracy

The morning in September 1963 when a corpse was found near the Corsican port of Propriano had followed a night of violent weather. All along the rocky, indented west coast from Ajaccio, birthplace of Napoleon Bonaparte, to the beautiful Golfe de Valinco, houses, people and livestock had been shaken by the elements on the rampage.

The months of July and August that year had been even hotter than usual; temperatures in the thirties had given rise to several electrical storms which sent locals and visitors alike scurrying to find shelter. The coast was twice whipped by the frenzy of a *Maestral* – the Corsican version of the Mistral – blowing from the north-east; and on the evening before the discovery of the body, a Tramontane, a dry, cold wind strong enough to blow a man off his feet, had swept down the valley into Propriano.

It had been a night, the locals would say later, when only the Devil and those with evil intent in their hearts would have been out of their beds. It was also the moment when the most mysterious and brutal murder associated with Rommel's Gold took place.

This story that was to thrust the area into the headlines and demonstrate once again that serious criminals were intent on finding the lost hoard, began in Propriano, a little harbour town tucked into the narrowest part of the Golfe de Valinco. A natural port, it has been in use ever since the days of the ancient Greeks who first enslaved the islanders in 565 BC. They were followed by the Carthaginians and Romans; then, in the eighteenth century, Propriano became a prime target for the Saracen pirates who largely destroyed it.

In the years that followed, the port was used only by local fishermen until the twentieth century. In the early 1900s it was redeveloped and turned into a thriving marina which today is used by French ferries from Toulon and Marseilles and a variety of vessels from nearby Sardinia. During the German and Italian occupation of Corsica, Propriano was utilised by the Axis forces. It was bombed by Allied aircraft on several occasions and a number of the terminal buildings were sabotaged by resistance fighters before the island was set free.

The area around Propriano is, indeed, historically steeped in bloodshed. Battles have been waged hereabouts by forces of Greeks, Romans, Vandals, Byzantines, Saracens and Genoese. France finally took control in 1769 when her troops defeated Pascal Paoli, the first independent ruler of Corsica, at Ponte Nuovo, by so doing ending a decade of self-rule and heralding continuous French government, only interrupted by the Axis forces' occupation during 1942–43. Despite the long period of French rule, some areas of the island feel more Italian than French. Certainly the Italian influence is very much in evidence on the west coast – especially in and around Propriano.

In recent years the town has grown in importance, largely under the direction of a powerful coalition consisting of the mayor, a second-generation Italian immigrant named Emile Mocchi, his nephew, one of the leaders of a prominent nationalist group, and southern Corsica's most renowned 'godfather', Jean-Jerome (aka 'Jean-Je') Colonna, veteran of the notorious French Connection. Together, it is said, this alliance of unlikely bedfellows has largely held in check power struggles between the area's political and Mafia organisations, which between them have held sway for several generations – although reports of mob and nationalist violence still continue to crop up regularly in the media.

The area has another claim to fame. Already in 1839, Propser Mérimée, who lived for a time on the island, had written *Colomba*, which has been called the first 'realistic' novel about the Corsican way of life. And it was here in the summer of 1841 that the great French novelist, Alexandre Dumas *père*, while on holiday, wrote his renowned novel of violence and intimidation, *The Corsican Brothers*. The anonymous translator of the first English edition in 1844 pointed out to his readers that the book was no mere invention, but based on fact.

'The story of *The Corsican Brothers* is written in an easy, sketchy style,' the man wrote, 'presenting on one side an interesting picture of the habits, prejudices and superstitions of the Corsicans, and particularly of the "Vendetta", or war of vengeance, carried on between families and connections, sometimes for several generations.'

Dumas's tale of the bandit-ridden island and its feuding people was evidently drawn from his own research and for the first time depicted a Corsican way of life few were aware of. The novel greatly enhanced its author's reputation and the ingenuity of the plot and sensation of the vendetta would in time make it ideal material for films, radio and television.

The most famous cinema version still remains the 1941 adaptation starring Douglas Fairbanks Jr who, in an early example of split-screen filming, played both the leading roles. Because of the wartime occupation the film had, in fact, only recently been seen on the island when a brutalised body, similar to one described by Dumas in the story, was found on that September morning on the Col de Santa Giulia.

According to tradition, September is the month for guns in Corsica. The local men who have spent the summer dreaming of stalking on the *maquis* – the brush-like vegetation that covers the island – begin their hunting for wild boars. The hunt has a dual purpose: it keeps down the population of boars while providing a very tasty meal. The meat of the Corsican wild boar – known as the *sanglier* – is dark in colour and more aromatic than that of others of the species because the animal feeds on the *maquis*.

A group of three hunters who set off from Propriano on that September morning were already dreaming of plates of the steaming dark meat as they climbed up into the foothills, guns at the ready. What they had not bargained for was the contorted human corpse that one of the men stumbled over in the undergrowth. Charles Van Deusen described the discovery in an article published in October 1963:

> A man was killed a few weeks ago on the island of Corsica. He had been frequenting local bars, boasting that he had discovered the fabled sunken treasure of General Erwin Rommel. After a couple of nights of such behaviour, his bullet-ridden body turned up in a field near Propriano.

So far, the police have caught nobody. Yet few Corsicans have any doubt about the identity of the murderer or murderers. Their collective name is being whispered all over the island – *The Mafia*!

It took the local police several days to identify the body after it had been transported to the mortuary in Propriano. The man's name was given as André Mattei, a professional diver in his thirties, from Marseilles. Mattei was said to have learned his underwater skills during military service with the French Navy and then turned his training into a commercial activity. He had apparently helped salvage a number of wrecks around the Mediterranean before arriving in Corsica in the summer of 1963.

Details of Mattei's life on the island are sketchy. It is said he was interested in treasure hunting and offered his services to anyone looking for Rommel's Gold, but got no response and so made a number of dives himself off the east coast around Bastia. What he evidently had not learned was to take special care when getting involved with the lost treasure. Whether there was any truth in André Mattei's claim to have found the location of the lost hoard, his death prevented any chance to put it to the test. As the local edition of *Paris-Presse* reported: 'Full particulars of Mattei's death have not been released, if they have been found at all.'

One element of the killing that surprised investigators was the place where the body had been found. There was no doubt that if Rommel's Gold was anywhere, it was off the *east* coast. As far as anyone knew, Mattei had never strayed far from Bastia, so why should his body have been found on the opposite side of the island? Had the diver been murdered in the field at

Propriano, people wondered, or killed in one of his usual haunts and his body taken across country to avoid the obvious association with the treasure and the possibility he may actually have found something?

One inhabitant of Bastia who had been drinking with Mattei shortly before his death told *Paris-Presse* that the diver claimed to have heard about people who became interested in the treasure and then died mysteriously – usually from 'falls from a great height'. Such suggestions about Mattei's death naturally heightened speculation, as Van Deusen reported: 'If the whispers are correct, then this is not the first time on which the Mafia has displayed its interest in the tantalising cache of loot. Others are said to have vanished into the thin Corsican air after making the mistake of babbling about the treasure.' The journalist concluded that the young Frenchman's death gave rise to three interesting possibilities:

1. That he had actually found the treasure, only to have the knowledge fatally prised out of him.
2. That the Mafia, perhaps with his help, had secretly raised the sunken cases – or some of them – and were anxious to prevent anyone else from poking around to verify the fact.
3. That the Mafia, having so far failed to find the treasure, were intent on keeping all other searchers away.*

---

* It has also been suggested that André Mattei may have been a French spy trying to get information on the Mafia and used the treasure story as bait knowing it would get back to the criminals. Richard Deacon in his book, *The French Secret Service* (1990), mentions an André Mattei who worked for the country's intelligence bureau in the 1960s. However, it is unlikely they are one and the same person; this Mattei had been head of a French diplomatic mission to Egypt who was arrested on charges of espionage in 1961. It took over a year of intense diplomatic pressure by the French government to gain his release.

In fact, the Mafia was just one of several shadowy organisations in Corsica who were all very interested in locating the missing gold.

From the information I have gathered, it seems clear that a number of illegal organisations regarded the finding of Rommel's treasure as an ideal way of helping to finance their nefarious operations. Foremost among these are the Corsican Mafia, the Union Corse and one of the separatist groups, the Corsican National Liberation Front, or FLNC.

Each of these groups has a history of violence and it is not difficult to understand why they might have devoted time and energy to trying to locate the Nazi hoard that was believed to lie so close at hand.

The first of this trio, the Corsican Mafia, is, rather different from the large, formal criminal organisation of the same name that operates in Sicily and America. It is a smaller syndicate of criminals that has evolved out of the ancient traditions of family honour and revenge on the island, the same traditions so well described by Dumas and Mérimée.

For centuries, short tempers, lack of forgiveness and long memories have been characteristic of the people of Corsica. Any man who laid a finger on another man's daughter, it was said, faced marriage...or instant death. The punishment for touching another man's wife, carried no such option – death by shooting was mandatory. And all the time the law – such as it was – turned a blind eye.

Corsica became known as the home of the vendetta. These family 'wars' were particularly prevalent in the south-west of the island, especially around the town of Sartene, which is only a short distance inland from Propriano.

The feuds could start in the most innocuous way – a drunken insult, a lost animal, even a tree hanging over a neighbour's boundary. No matter what, honour had to be served and the price was death by knife, bullet, mutilation or even being burned alive.

In turn, each death had to be paid back – and so the vendettas between families began. The victim's nearest relative was bound by the unwritten code to kill either the murderer or another male member of his family. The responsibility of avenging the family's honour then fell on the shoulders of the latest victim's closest male relative.

The responsibility for revenge could go all the way down to third cousins and frequently continued for generations. It was said that no man was worthy of the name until he had killed another man.

Historical archives in Corsica reveal that the vendetta was at its height in the late seventeenth and early eighteenth century, when almost 1,000 lives were being taken every year. The number decreased throughout the nineteenth century, and instances of such family 'wars' have been few in number since the middle of the twentiety century. Feuds do undoubtedly continue today and can be just as bloody. However, these have become so mixed up with the rivalries of the separatist factions that it is said to be almost impossible to differentiate between those that are part of the demand for self-rule for Corsica and acts of Mafia-style revenge.

The Corsican Mafia evolved naturally from this tradition, emerging in recognisable form in the early 1920s. Although it never attempted to become a formal organisation in the manner of the Sicilian and American mafia groups, it did develop its own special identity and – shades of the old vendettas – began imposing death sentences on those who gave information to outsiders.

Rumour has it that the 'home town' of the early Corsican 'godfathers' was a small village in the mountains near the town of Bonifacio, a huddle of ancient buildings on top of the high cliffs that form the southernmost point of the island. It is said that the Guerini family are the island's leading Mafia clan. According to an American historian, Alfred W McCoy, who has made a study of the organisation, a man who is accepted as an ordinary gangster by the Corsicans is 'in the *milieu*', while a respected syndicate boss is known as *'un vrai Monsieur'*. The most senior are known as *Paceri* or 'Peacemakers' as they have the power to impose discipline on members and mediate in vendettas.

While it is generally agreed that most mafiosi in Sicily and America seem to have a limited number of refined criminal skills beyond the violence associated with orchestrating vice, prostitution and bootlegging, their Corsican brothers have a long record of successful smuggling, counterfeiting and art theft, alongside the manufacture and smuggling of drugs.

During the early years of its existence, the Corsican Mafia worked hard to spread its net beyond the narrow confines of the island, setting up operations in North Africa, the Middle East and later even Latin America, all the time keeping one step ahead of the law enforcement agencies in these countries. The group proved to be particular experts at making heroin, choosing to manufacture the drug in clandestine laboratories in France, especially Marseilles. Soon this teeming port that has been for centuries the crossroads of France's empire – as well as a stronghold of working-class militancy – became the capital of its underworld: the Chicago of France, in fact.

The power of the Corsican Mafia in Marseilles made them a force to be reckoned with, and the corrupt politicians and foreign powers who subsequently ruled the city all had to deal with them. First, the French Fascists employed the Corsicans to battle with Communist demonstrators in the 1930s. Next, during the German occupation, the Gestapo used them to spy on the Communist underground. And then, as the war reached a crucial stage in 1943, the Corsicans found themselves being courted by the Americans as the Allies prepared to invade Sicily.

The Sicilian Mafia, it was reported, had at that time been 'severely repressed' by Mussolini. (It would not, in fact, regain its power until 1950.) The American Operations Support Squadron – which became the CIA in 1947 – wanted to recruit waterfront workers in Sicily to report on enemy activities prior to the Allied landings.

So who better to arrange this than the Corsicans who had for years co-operated with their fellow criminals just 300 miles away across the Mediterranean? There were striking similarities between the two nationalities to explain this mutuality: both inhabited arid, mountainous islands, shared a fierce pride in honour and had a heritage of bloody family vendettas.

Naturally, the Corsican 'godfather', Antoine Guerini, demanded a price from the OSS for his co-operation. His organisation was to be allowed to continue using Marseilles for its heroin operation uninterrupted. This agreement was to have far-ranging implications, especially when the conflict ended. An agreement between the Corsicans and the Mafia drug dealers in the US would result in the nation being swamped with hard drugs in a way no one could have imagined when the wartime deal was struck. (According to one estimate, by 1965 the Corsican Mafia had two dozen labs in Marseilles exporting nearly five tons of heroin to the US every year.)

In the aftermath of the German defeat, the Corsican Mafia redoubled its activities in Marseilles, setting up more heroin laboratories both in the city's slum tenements and in luxurious villas in the surrounding countryside. During the late 1940s, the group made a fortune in the Indochina War by smuggling gold bullion and paper currency between Saigon and Marseilles. The following decade they instigated a hugely successful black market in tax-free cigarettes, smuggling American brands from North Africa into Europe.

All this expansion naturally required a constant supply of fresh capital. And when the first rumours of Rommel's Gold began to circulate on the island, there seems little doubt that the Mafia bosses sat up and took notice. Experience had already taught them the value of fine art, and the descriptions of the Nazi gold, silver and precious artefacts worth millions added up to the kind of haul that *vrai Monsieur* Guerini and his men could put to good use. Certainly, no one else was going to get to it first.

But if, as the rumours suggested, the Corsican Mafia was responsible for the death of André Mattei, further evidence suggests that any information the diver may have possessed did not enable them to find the treasure. A newspaper report the following year in May 1964 reported a pitched battle on the Bastia sands between two groups of men, in all probability mafiosi and the local police.

The story in the Marseilles daily, *L'Antenne*, headlined BATTLE ON CORSICAN BEACH, described the encounter between the two groups late one night on the sands near the River Golo. The police had apparently received a tip-off that a group of men were behaving strangely near Cap Sud and had arrived to find the men about to set sail in a small cruiser. The report stated:

> When the officers approached the men, they were greeted by gunfire, In the subsequent shoot-out, several people were injured including two of the intruders. Three others made their escape in the sand dunes.
>
> The two injured men were taken to Bastia where they were identified as members of a *well-known criminal gang* [my italics]. The police are declining to give any further details until charges have been made, but our reporter understands the men may have been on an expedition to try and find Rommel's Treasure which has been in the news again recently.

In fact, no charges were made and nothing further was heard of the incident. Although many Corsicans who read about the events agreed the men were almost certainly gangsters, there was another possibility. Perhaps the equally notorious Union Corse was also after the hoard?

Unlike the Corsican Mafia, the Union Corse cannot be simply categorised as a criminal organisation. While it undoubtedly is involved in crime and illegal activities throughout Europe and North America, it is also claimed to be a society woven together by extensive and close family links and by a powerful feeling of obligation.

The French writer Pierre Nathan has perhaps best summed up the group, as 'a brotherhood of people turned on by the same criminal ideas who freely form alliances and partnerships and who just as freely dissolve them. They welcome on an equal footing members of Armenian, Turkish and Lebanese origins as well as any French thief, forger or con-man likely to be of use.'

The group also has 'separatist-nationalist' ambitions, according to Nathan, and strives for the day when Corsica is no longer governed from France. It has funded its activities to achieve this end from a diversity of sources and the allure of Rommel's Gold was every bit as attractive to the Union Corse as to its rivals in the Mafia.

The origins of the Union Corse are lost in the past, but most experts believe that it has been in existence longer than the Unione Siciliano – as the Mafia was originally known. Although springing from the same bloody tradition and bound together by the same code of honour, it has for many years had a base in France and furthered its criminal activities in many of the nation's colonies.

Protection rackets, prostitution, smuggling and the suppression of rival gangs head the Union Corse's list of priorities. For much of the time it has lived in an uneasy alliance with the various mafia groups enjoying the same rich spoils. Only on issues affecting Corsica has there been the occasional outbreak of hostility to one another – much to the satisfaction of the law agencies thereby provided with a brief respite from pursuing them both.

Ian Fleming was just one of a number of writers who was aware of the the Union Corse's interest in the treasure trove off Bastia when he used the facts in *On Her Majesty's Secret Service*. Unfortunately, he gave no further details in the book or to me during our meeting. However, stories repeated by Corsican journalists suggest that Union Corse members carried out searches for Rommel's Gold in the late forties, fifties and mid-sixties. One of these is linked to the Yugoslav investigator Jakov Jovanovic, murdered in Lyons in 1947.

It may well be no more than a conspiracy theory, but it is said that Jovanovic became a high-profile target for the criminal organisation after his investigations about the treasure trove in Corsica. Whether or not he gave any information to his killer in that backwater of the Rhône – or even if the hit man was in the employ of the Union Corse – has proved impossible to substantiate. But whispers that a very secretive exploration was carried out not long after Jovanovic's murder persisted for years.

Less shrouded in theory and mystery were the stories told in 1965 by people living near Cap Sud about a large fishing boat exploring the estuary. A team of divers were seen going overboard at one spot for days on end before the vessel finally weighed anchor and returned to Bastia. The ownership of the boat was apparently known to some of these men and women, but not one was prepared to say a word to the authorities, '*ayant peur de l'Union*'.

Aside from the Corsican Mafia and the Union Corse, one of the island's major separatist groups, the Front de Libération National Corse (FLNC), is also believed to have considered looking for Rommel's Gold. Founded in 1976 and modelled on the Algerian FLN, it is one of several subversive groups that emerged during this period including A Cuncolta Naziunalista, l'Action Régionaliste Corse, and le Parti du Peuple. All are categorised by bloodshed, according to the Corsican historian, C X Culioli: 'Their violence cannot be separated from the lawlessness that has been endemic on the island for centuries, with bloody conflicts between north and south and among various mafia-type organisations.'

Like all its rivals, the FLNC requires funding. Stories on the island talk of the collection of a 'revolutionary tax' – money resulting from armed robbery and bank jobs. Some of this loot has been invested in local real estate and in gambling operations on Corsica and abroad in Italy and Africa. Criminal-style operations have been carried out involving drugs, weapons and money laundering. Corruption, too, has been employed to tie high-ranking politicians into the separatists' networks.

According to the Corsican police, in the course of the 1990s most of the original fighters left the separatists to be replaced by purely criminal elements. And in 1995, for example, on average one assassination attempt was carried out on Corsica *every day*. There is also evidence that when a senior official of the FLNC heard rumours about the interest of his rivals in Rommel's Gold, a directive went out to members on the east coast to keep a watch on such activities. If anyone else found the treasure they were not to hesitate to seize it.

In 1998, Jean-Michael Rossi and François Santoni, two men who had been deeply involved in the nationalist movement for years, published a sensational exposé, *Pour solde de tout compte*. In this book they denounced their former allies as 'a mafia that increasingly obeys criminal rather than political motives' and revealed the names of a number of leading members of the underground movement. Rossi, the ex-leader of the shadowy A Cuncolta, and Santoni, a former official known as 'The Iguana', had announced plans to throw more light on the fund-raising activities of the FLNC and at least seven other different terrorist organisations in Corsica in a second book. Neither lived long enough to carry out this ambition.

Rossi was cut down by hitmen in a small village near Bonifacio in August 1999 and Santoni died in August 2001 in a hail of bullets as he walked to his car after a wedding reception in Monacia-d'Aullene. Both were on private visits to remote areas and despite being accompanied by bodyguards were mown down by assault rifles in what local police described as 'audacious mafia-style hits in the heart of their southern fiefdom'.

The gunmen have as yet not been identified but are believed to be professionals because of the carefully planned manner of the killings. The police, though, suspect the involvement of mafiosi, and were given a chilling reminder of the old days of the vendetta when an anonymous telephone caller threatened more killings to avenge the assassinations.

The murders of Rossi and Santoni represent the latest names that must be added to the list of crime-related deaths associated with the search for Rommel's Gold. And with their murders another chapter comes to an end in the continuing mystery of the missing loot. Today, though, sixty years after the story began, we can be sure of three things: where the treasure originated, how it was moved, and where it is located.

During the writing of this book, I have sailed along the eastern coast of Corsica in the wake of Peter Fleig, Louis Bordes, Henri Helle, Stewart Pears, Edwin Link and all the other treasure hunters seeking the elusive six chests. I remain as convinced today as the very first day I began my research that the hoard *does* exist and the fortune in gold, silver, diamonds and precious artefacts is still there beneath the sun-dappled waves awaiting a claimant.

Epilogue

There is one further curious episode in the mystery of Rommel's Gold that should be told. It concerns another former German soldier who has claimed to know the exact whereabouts of the buried treasure. Yet although this man has spoken to at least two writers in recent years, his story is full of discrepancies – unintentional or deliberate – while his subsequent disappearance has thrown a question mark over both the facts he has given and even the identity of the man himself. First, the consistent details such as they are known.

The man's name is Walter Kirn and when last seen in the 1990s he was living near Freiburg, a medieval town perched on the western slopes of the Black Forest, once one of the wildest stretches of countryside in Europe. He claims to have been a member of the SS firing squad that executed Captain Ludwig Dahl and the three other officers for dereliction of duty. On the dead body of one of the men, he says, he found a hand-drawn plan of the precise location of Rommel's Gold.

According to Kirn he was born in Hamburg in 1923. His father was an engineer and in his teens Walter was apprenticed as a metal turner. Like many other young men of the time his

205

imagination was caught by the rise of Hitler and on the outbreak of war he joined the SS. Kirn served in Poland and Russia – where he was badly scarred in battle and received a medal for bravery – before being promoted an *Oberscharführer* (Staff Sergeant) and posted to Italy in 1943. Here he claimed to have been given a special assignment confiscating gold bars, silverware, precious stones and artworks required to finance the cost of the war.

In the last week of September 1943, he was ordered to Massa for the less than pleasant duty of taking charge of a firing squad. He knew only the basic facts about the four men he was to shoot – that they had misappropriated valuables destined for Berlin and been condemned to death.

After the firing squad had carried out their duty, it fell to Kirn to check that all four were dead. While inspecting the body of Captain Dahl he said he noticed a piece of paper pushed down inside one of the officer's leather boots. Removing the sheet, he saw that it was a map of Corsica with a spot carefully marked off the east coast. Walter Kirn was in no doubt it had to be a map of the place where the men had hidden their stolen booty. It took him only a moment longer to decide to keep the information to himself.

Thereafter the war took its inevitable course. Following the collapse of Italy, Kirn was reassigned to Austria. On 18 September 1944 he was wounded again and saw out the remainder of the conflict in a military hospital at Salzburg. When the Third Reich finally fell to the Allied and Russian forces in 1945, he was taken prisoner and placed in the Dachau internment camp. Later he was released and returned to life in the beaten and divided country of his birth. It is at this point in

Walter Kirn's story that the facts become confused through a combination of his different versions of events and a series of rumours.

The sequence begins in 1988 when he met the German novelist Gunter Seuren at Titisee-Neustadt, a health resort in the upper Black Forest. There, apparently in a mood of confession, he told the author that far from finding out about the treasure from a map, he had actually been ordered to *collect* it from Corsica. He had been sent there on 12 September 1943 disguised as a sailor by an SS officer, *Obersturmführer* Buhler. Kirn said he believed Buhler was acting on behalf of higher-ranking officers in the SS who, fearing the war was going to be lost, wanted the valuables to provide for their futures. When he reached Corsica, however, the treasure was already on the bottom of the ocean.

Seuren, however, was far from convinced that Kirn was telling the truth – nor was he the only writer to think so. A French author, Michel Bagnaud, who had made something of a speciality of writing books on treasure hunting – including a best-seller, *Les Chasseurs d'Eldorado* – went to see the former soldier in Freiburg in 1990 and came away equally puzzled by another revisionist version of events.

Again, Kirn said he had been a member of the SS. But it was while he was taking part in the Ardennes offensive that the crucial event in his story of the lost treasure occurred. There he had come across two badly injured soldiers: Captain Dahl, who already appeared dead, and another soldier who was seriously wounded, but still conscious. The soldier told Kirn he hoped the advancing Americans would find him and treat him for his injuries. He begged Kirn to take some documents he had in his possession back to Germany and 'give them to my family in Romberg.'

Kirn told Bagnaud that his curiosity had got the better of him and he had opened the documents, to find that one was a map of a cache of loot buried off the coast of Corsica. Shortly after the war, he had mounted an expedition to the island but had been unable to find anything.

Although Kirn offered his interviewer the co-ordinates and bearings of the site, Bagnaud remained suspicious as he wrote the following year in an article 'Profession: Inventor of Treasure' for the May issue of *VSD* magazine. How, he asked, could someone who had been an officer in a proscribed organisation like the SS have been released from prison so soon after the end of the war? And why, if he was so sure of the location, had he so singularly failed to find the loot?

Despite his reservations, Bagnaud did try looking for Rommel's Gold. The location was somewhat to the north of the generally accepted dumping ground, and although the French treasure hunter reported in one particular area an 'abnormality of the magnetic meter at a depths of 75 metres' it was not enough to encourage any further exploration. Bagnaud left Corsica convinced the information was just another deception by Kirn to protect his secret... if he had one at all.

However, Walter Kirn was not quite finished talking – there was yet another version of events. This story began in the internment camp at Dachau where Kirn was alleged to have met a high-rank SS Officer named Schmidt, who had once been a secretary to Heinrich Himmler. Allegedly, Schmidt knew that he would be sentenced to death for his war crimes and offered Kirn a fortune to lend him his clothes. He could then go to work outside the camp as Kirn did each day and escape. The 'inducements' he offered were the whereabouts of some valuable paintings in Austria, a vast collection of gold coins in Italy... and the location of Rommel's Gold. No sooner had Kirn agreed and Schmidt handed over the details, than the SS officer was suddenly transferred to another camp before the escape could take place.

Improbability now piles on improbability. Kirn is alleged to have offered *two* of the fortunes to an American officer, Major Breitenbach, who was in charge of the camp, in return for his freedom. He kept the details of the Corsican hoard to himself.

Breitenbach accepted, so the story goes. In Austria, apparently, he successfully recovered a number of valuable pictures, but arrived too late at a grotto in Massarossa near Viareggio where there was every sign that looters had beaten him to the gold coins. Still, the Major kept his side of the bargain and set Kirn free with a passport in the name of another man. Despite the ingenuity of this story, there are no records I have been able to trace of an American Major Breitenbach or his recovery of any German loot.

There are also rumours that Walter Kirn paid several visits to Corsica, the first time under the auspices of the French government during which time he quarrelled with the salvage experts over the amount of his fee. As a result he became vague about the site and also got himself into trouble for stealing an underwater camera to pay off some debts.

On another occasion Kirn is said to have 'co-operated' with the Mafia in a search – although whether willingly or unwillingly is not stated – and left the island in a hurry when it ended in failure. A further report claims that he made one final attempt in June 1975 in partnership with a German nautical firm, Klaus F Keppler. The team used the very latest underwater technology, but again without any success.

Since then, Walter Kirn has been variously reported living in Frankfurt, Munich and, most recently, the Black Forest. He is said to be in poor health and has no further intention of looking for the treasure – or discussing it with anyone.

Which brings me to perhaps the most remarkable theory of all: that the man who may be living in seclusion amid the glorious forestry of the *Schwarzwald* is someone we have met time and again in the pages of this book. Consider, if you will, the uncanny similarities between Walter Kirn and the person who has haunted this mystery since it began on that September morning sixty years ago and ask yourself if they could be one and the same person?

The man known as Peter Fleig.

Sources

Books

Barclay, Brigadier C N, *Against Great Odds.* Sifton Praed & Co, 1955

Bryce, Ivar, *You Only Live Twice.* Weidenfeld & Nicolson, 1975

Cockerill, A W, *Sir Percy Sillitoe.* W H Allen, 1975

Churchill, Winston S, *The Second World War.* Cassell & Company, 1950

Deacon, Richard, *The French Secret Service.* Grafton, 1990

Douglas-Home, Charles, *Rommel.* Weidenfeld & Nicolson, 1973

Eton, Peter & Leasor, James, *Conspiracy of Silence.* Angus & Robertson, 1960

Fraser, David, *Knight's Cross: A Life of Field Marshal Erwin Rommel.* HarperCollins, 1993

Gordon, Donald, *The Golden Oyster.* William Morrow & Co., 1968

Hoek, Susan van, *From Sea to Sky.* Best Publishing Company, 1993

Irving, David, *The Trail of the Fox.* Bookthrift Co., 1977

Jaeger, Charles de, *The Linz File.* Webb & Bower, 1981

Landsborough, Gordon, *Tobruk Commando*. Cassell & Company, 1956

Lewin, Ronald, *Rommel As Military Commander*. Hart-Davis, 1968

Ling, Dwight L, *Tunisia: From Protectorate to Republic*. Indiana University, 1967

Lycett, Andrew, *Ian Fleming*. Weidenfeld & Nicolson, 1995

McCormick, Donald, *17F: The Life of Ian Fleming*. Peter Owen, 1993

Memmi, Albert, *La statue de sel*. Plon, 1954

Moorehead, Alan, *The March To Tunis*. Harper & Rowe Inc., 1943

Moss, W Stanley, *Gold Is Where You Hide It*. André Deutsch Ltd, 1956

Nicholas, Lynn H, *The Rape of Europa*. Macmillan, 1994

Pearson, John, *The Life of Ian Fleming*. Jonathan Cape, 1966

Roxan, David & Wanstall, Ken, *The Jackdaw of Linz*. Cassell & Company Ltd, 1964

Sillitoe, Percy, *Clock Without Dagger*. Cassell, 1955

Smith, Sir Sidney, *Mostly Murder*. Companion Book Club, 1961

Stenuit, Robert, *Ces mondes secrets ou j'ai plongé*. Robert Laffont, 1988

Vacha, Robert, *A Spy For Churchill*. Everest Books, 1974

Young, Desmond, *Rommel. Harrap*, 1950

Newspapers and Documents
Daily Mail
Daily Telegraph
Diver
Glasgow Herald

Sources

L'Antenne
L'Espoir de Nice
L'Intransigeant
Le Monde
Mail on Sunday
National Geographic
New Scientist
Nice-Matin
Observer
Paris-Presse
Smithsonian Magazine
Sussex Express & County Herald
Sunday Telegraph
Sunday Times
The Times
True Magazine
Twickenham & Whitton Chronicle

National Archives, Kew; British Musem, London; Bundesarchiv, Germany; Library of Congress, Washington; Binghamton University, USA; British Newspaper Library, Colindale and The London Library.

Index

215